MARTIN ROACH

TAKE THAT

NOW AND THEN: THE ILLUSTRATED STORY

UNOFFICIAL

HarperCollins*Publishers*

HarperCollins*Publishers*
77–85 Fulham Palace Road,
Hammersmith, London W6 8JB

www.harpercollins.co.uk

First published by HarperCollins*Publishers* 2006
This updated edition 2009

10 9 8 7 6 5 4 3 2 1

A catalogue record of this book is
available from the British Library

ISBN 978-0-00-731845-2

Printed and bound in Great Britain by
Butler Tanner & Dennis Ltd, Frome, Somerset

This book is dedicated to my father Tony, who is the greatest man to ever walk this earth.

He has given me everything, showed me how to live and set an example that I will always strive to meet.

If I live to be a thousand years old, I will never forget.

For you, Dad.

Martin Roach
May 2009

CONTENTS

FOREWORD
BY LOUIS WALSH

Take that were the best boy band in the world. They were the reason I started Boyzone – Boyzone were the Irish Take That. I thought Gary and the band were absolutely brilliant. They appealed to everybody, their records were great and they had everything: great ballads, great up-tempo numbers, amazing live shows – I saw them at The Point in Dublin and the sound, the lights, the choreography, the entire show was just amazing.

Then, of course, you had Nigel Martin-Smith, who did a fantastic job managing them. He made Take That special: people weren't always allowed near them, they weren't accessible everywhere, hanging out at nightclubs all the time with every Page Three girl, like so many boy bands today. Nigel made them special and that had an awful lot to do with their success.

Robbie has become successful and he is a great performer … a huge success. I admire his work ethic. He's a fantastic worker who knows how to appeal to both girls and boys. I have been known to criticize him, but he is so ambitious and I would never underestimate Robbie. He knows exactly what he is doing.

Meanwhile, Take That are still selling out stadiums, which is incredible. Their records are still on the radio, their first TV documentary was fantastic and they are still so popular. For me, they totally provided the blueprint for that genre.

They will always be England's best boy band.

Louis Walsh
February 2006

INTRODUCTION

WITHIN TWELVE MONTHS OF ANNOUNCING their 'reunion' tour in late 2005, Take That had completed the biggest comeback in pop history. At the time of writing, they can boast the fastest-selling tour in British music history; they have topped the singles charts three more times and produced two of the biggest-selling albums of the last decade; their own TV specials enjoy some of the highest ratings for entertainment shows in years … it seems there is no limit to what they can now achieve.

HOW HAVE THEY DONE IT?

On the surface, there are three key reasons. Firstly, the cultural impact from their original career has proved to have far longer-lasting resonance than anyone – probably even the band themselves – realized. Pop is a fickle beast, and for a band in that genre to have any lasting validity is unusual. Take That was not a pioneering fashion band, far from it. They were not musical innovators. They were certainly not the critics' band of choice. Yet what the colossal success of their comeback tours tells us is that they clearly made an indelible mark on British music and cultural history. The broadsheets might not like to think so, but it is a fact. Among the thousands of bands that spilled out of the Nineties, the importance of the majority would fade with time. Take That's legacy, however, was clearly a sleeping giant.

This pop behemoth was first awakened by an ITV1 documentary and then established on the high streets of Britain by a series of comeback tours that captured the nation's imagination on an unprecedented scale. The band's famously energetic and explosive original live shows have been surpassed by new tours of stunning proportions. Filling some of the UK's biggest venues was one thing, entertaining the thousands in attendance quite another. They did both with aplomb. Why would so many hundreds of thousands of people chase tickets to see a band from their childhood? Partly because they wanted a good time; partly because the shows themselves were sensational; but mainly because, to millions of people, Take That matter.

'TO MILLIONS OF PEOPLE, TAKE THAT MATTER.'

Finally, the band have since produced two albums of new material that are genuinely polished, well-crafted and hugely popular. A live show alone does not qualify Take That for the accolade of pop's biggest comeback. Of course, nostalgia plays a part, but the band has brilliantly complemented this revival with a slew of superb new songs. Opening single 'Patience' was a new classic in the 'Back For Good' vein, while follow-up 'Shine' was an addictive curve-ball. Both were No. 1. The album, *Beautiful World*, silenced all but the very harshest of critics. And by proving they were no one-trick pony with the subsequent stunning No. 1 album *Circus* and its corresponding chart-topping single 'Greatest Day', Take That have now turned themselves from being the biggest comeback in British pop history into the biggest *contemporary* band in the country.

It is rare for a pop band to get a second bite of the cherry – rarer still for any comeback to have greater commercial potential than the first time around. That's what Take That appear to have done.

From childhood days in bedrooms writing songs, to thanking audiences of 60,000 in football stadiums over twenty years later, this is how it all happened …

Martin Roach
May 2009

A WISH AWAY

GARY BARLOW WAS WASHING HIS Ford Orion outside his parents' house when his mum shouted that someone was on the phone for him. It was a local model-agency owner called Nigel Martin-Smith whom Gary had been to see that very afternoon. The 19-year-old Gary had wanted to speak with Nigel about getting small acting roles now that he had an Equity card. At the end of their meeting, Gary had given Nigel a demo tape of some songs he'd been writing and recording in his bedroom.

Drying his hands, Gary picked up the phone.

'Hello Gary, it's Nigel Martin-Smith here. I've listened to that tape you gave me and I just wondered who is singing on it?'

'It's me, Nigel.'

'OK, but who is playing the music and made the arrangements and everything?'

Gary had been using the stage name of Kurtis Rush.

'I did, Nigel. I did it all in my bedroom.'

'Er … right. Can you come back to see me straight away, Gary? Tonight …'

At that precise moment, Take That, arguably the biggest British boy band ever, was born.

Regardless of Gary's latter-day solo success and irrespective of the public's perception of Take That's key players, it is a simple fact that the very heart of the band always was – and always will be – Gary Barlow. Of the thirty-three original tracks on the band's three studio albums, Gary was solely credited for writing twenty-five of them and co-writing a further seven.

Born on 20 January 1971, Gary shares his birthday with punk svengali and cultural icon Malcolm McLaren, twenty-five years his senior. He was brought up in Frodsham,

7

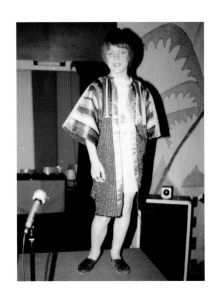

Cheshire, a small town with some big money, filled with sandstone brick buildings, a couple of housing estates, an old church, scatterings of hills and good walking country. It has been said that Frodsham people think they are a bit above their neighbours – and they are, overlooking as they do the chemical and petrol plants around Runcorn.

Gary was born to parents Marge and Colin Barlow, with one older brother, Ian (who now runs his own building firm). As a baby, Gary cried so much that his mother wondered if there was something seriously wrong with his health, but then they realized he was just a tiny baby who liked to make a lot of noise. His primary education was at Weaver Vale, where a final-year primary-school production of *Joseph and the Amazing Technicolor Dreamcoat* saw him take the lead role. However, the first real signs of a future life in entertainment came when Gary was just 11 years old and chose a keyboard for Christmas, having been given the choice of either that or a BMX bike. Remarkably – and there are numerous first-hand sources to back this up – the pre-teen Gary was very quickly writing his own material, and he remains entirely self-taught.

Gary's school life carried on at Frodsham High School, where his mother was a science technician. Perhaps surprisingly, given his young age, the schoolboy Gary had started performing professionally at social clubs in the local area. At this early stage, in true *Phoenix Nights* style, he incorporated a handful of jokes into his routine. Notably, his musical influences were generally older than those of most teens – although his first record was 'Living Next Door to Alice' by Smokie, he was a big Motown fan, and liked artists such as Elton John and Stevie Wonder. His main songwriting inspirations were The Beatles and Adam Ant, an odd mix but obviously not one that stifled his creativity.

As early as 13 Gary was playing solo every Saturday for £18 a night at Connahs Quay Labour Club in North Wales, performing classic working-men's standards such as 'Wind Beneath My Wings'. He'd been offered the job after coming second in a talent competition at the venue with a cover of the surreal classic, 'A Whiter Shade of Pale'. Gary's slot at the Labour Club lasted two years, during which time he also formed a duo with a friend known only as Heather. Together they played the pubs and clubs circuit for a further two years. He also formed a short-lived band inspired by Adam and the Ants. His rudimentary keyboard was soon replaced with a £600 organ with foot-pedals, which offered the budding songwriter far more musical possibilities.

One of the most significant early jobs he secured was a residency fronting a small,

middle-aged band at the Halton British Legion in Widnes, near Runcorn, which included four gigs every weekend until well after midnight. By then, the mid-teenage Gary was earning up to £140 a night, which was no small accomplishment, as well as supporting numerous working-men's club stars. Inevitably, late working hours and early school schedules were exhausting for him, but all he wanted to do was play and write and perform (and, according to sources at the Legion, eat Bacon Fries). He even gave up his beloved karate lessons because he broke his fingers twice and was concerned about jeopardizing his piano-playing.

Gary supported some notable performers, including Ken Dodd and Bobby Davro, and, perhaps more importantly, began to slip his original compositions into his set alongside the staple club standards. One of those original songs had taken him six minutes to write and was entitled 'A Million Love Songs'. Another two were called 'Another Crack in My Heart' and 'Why Can't I Wake Up with You?'.

By this stage, Gary would spend any spare time he had writing new material. In his own words, he 'wanted to be Seal'. On quiet weekends he'd aim to write and demo *one song a day* at home, a challenge he often completed. This prolific drive, cooped up in his bedroom, was balanced with the practical experience of weekly gigging. The Legion was an ideal sounding-board for his song ideas, and also a priceless three-year apprenticeship working with both the public and veteran musicians, especially for a boy who was still twelve months shy of taking his O levels when he started. The 'pie-and-mash circuit' might not be the most glamorous of jobs, but there is no better way to breed new talent.

It's hard to trace back to when a pop star has his first big break, but undoubtedly when Gary entered a song for the 1986 BBC Pebble Mill's competition 'A Song for Christmas', and promptly reached the semi-finals, it was a watershed moment. He was only 15. His mother had been largely unimpressed with his self-penned ballad 'Let's Pray for Christmas', but his music teacher entered it into the competition for him. Speaking on the TV documentary, *Take That: Where Did It All Go Right?*, the teacher, Mr Smiddy, said Gary was 'head and shoulders above the rest' of the music class he taught.

It was during a gym lesson that Mrs Nelson interrupted Gary to tell him he had been selected by the BBC to go into the next round of the seniors competition. This involved travelling down to London's West Heath Studios to record the track in full. It was the first time Gary had been inside a recording studio but he was a natural and made full use of the orchestra and backing vocalists on offer. The whole experience was filmed, and watching the clip now it is hard to imagine that Gary was only four years away from starting the biggest boy band of the Nineties. Although Gary's track stalled at the semi-finals stage, he won a modest amount of prize money (supplemented by selling cassettes of the song for 50p each back at school), which he promptly utilized by going into 10CC's Strawberry Studios in Stockport to demo some more of his own material.

During his time in London, Gary had met several famous agents and music-business executives, so his showbiz networking had begun. However, his path to stardom was far from smooth. Eager to win a potentially lucrative publishing deal – effectively selling his songs for other performers to sing – Gary scoured London's record labels looking for someone who thought he was capable of writing a smash hit for their artists. Among the usual polite rejections, Gary tells a story about one executive who listened to 'A Million Love Songs', scornfully ripped the tape out of the machine and slung it through the open window into the street, ending his bizarre tantrum with the warning that Gary should never darken his door again. Gary has, over the years, resisted what must be the great temptation to reveal this executive's name.

Meanwhile, Gary's secondary education was unremarkable, with no major dramas: he was a good student and passed six O levels, with his parents keen for him to work in banking or the police force.

Given their roles in Take That, it is interesting to note that two of the first members to start the chain of events leading to the band's formation were Howard and Jason. The oldest of the band, Howard Paul Donald, was born on 28 April 1968 in Droylsden, Manchester (Howard is almost six years older than the baby of the band, Robbie Williams). Howard was from a large family, with three brothers (Michael, Colin and

Glenn) and a sister (Samantha), as well as his father Keith and mother Kathleen. Both parents were entertainers, Keith teaching Latin American dance and Kathleen being a gifted singer. His parents later separated and he is also close to his step dad, Mike.

Surprisingly, Howard's first ambition was to be an airline pilot. He went to Moreside Junior School for his primary education, where reports suggest he was a good student.

His time there was not without its dramas though: 'A couple of weeks after I started school, I got this disease called impetigo. When I was off school, this teacher put a big sign on my desk saying "Don't Go Near This Desk!" When I told my mum, she drove up to the school and went mad!'

Howard's first album was by Adam Ant and, like his future band-mate Gary Barlow, he was a big fan of the Dandy Highwayman. However, as his teenage years rolled by he became fascinated with an altogether different style of music – breakbeat and hip hop. In turn, this relatively new genre introduced him to dancing – breakdancing in particular – and with this new obsession came a declining interest in academic matters.

'SURPRISINGLY, HOWARD'S FIRST AMBITION WAS TO BE AN AIRLINE PILOT.'

Breakdancing is an extraordinarily athletic and acrobatic style of movement and dance, that at the time was a central part of hip-hop culture, emerging as it did out of that movement in the South Bronx of New York City during the late Seventies and early Eighties. It can actually be traced back to 1969, when James Brown's 'Get on the Good Foot' inspired famously acrobatic dance moves, and simultaneously Afrika Bambaataa started organizing one of the first breakdance crews, The Zulu Kings. The relevance to Take That might seem tenuous, but by the early to mid Eighties hip hop and breakdancing had been exported across the Atlantic and imposed itself on the daily lives of British youth. School yards were filled with teenagers spinning on old pieces of lino, hip-hop clothing labels were worn and breakbeat music blared out of oversized ghetto blasters – suburban Britain doesn't have too many ghettos like the Bronx, but that wasn't the point. It was a style, a look and a sound that became immensely popular. Howard was exactly this type of breakdancing Brit, and he lived for it; he also listened to house music such as 808 State and even more experimental-

ist tracks by the likes of Kraftwerk, but hip hop was his first love. He often played truant so he could practise his moves, which increasingly included complex gymnastics, so that by the time he was 15 he was a very adept dancer indeed. According to an interview with Rick Sky for *The Take That Fact File* (Rick was one of the few writers to have covered the band from before they were famous), he once absconded from school for five weeks in a row: 'I only intended to have a few days off, but I kept taking another day, then another day, till the days had run into weeks. I got into awful trouble for that.' He later admitted to being caught graffitiing a bus, although that appears to be the extent of his waywardness. Like Gary, he also bought an electronic keyboard, but his main passion was always for dancing.

Despite his latter-day persona as the quietest member of Take That, Howard was something of an extrovert at school – breakdancing was hardly the domain of the class nerd, after all. This obviously provided plenty of distraction, because he left school without a single O level to his name. He wasn't altogether troubled by that, not least because he had just been enrolled in a local breakdancing crew called the RDS Royals.

It was 1986 and Britain was in the grip of the Thatcher years. Unemployment was over the 3 million mark, social unrest was rife and many people, particularly the young and less privileged, were isolated and disillusioned. Behind all the politics and histrionics, the reality for 16-year-olds with no qualifications, like Howard, was simple:

either unemployment or the last bastion of state-sponsored slave labour, the Youth Training Scheme, or YTS. Howard did a few modelling jobs and also took a job painting cars for £40 a week – he was still working on cars when he first auditioned for Take That.

He started to supplement his feeble income by dancing on podiums and stages at clubs such as Manchester's Apollo, to vibe the crowd up. It was an ideal way of getting paid to practise and, besides, if he wasn't working at these clubs he would have been there as a paying punter anyway. Consequently he developed a very muscular physique at an early age, leading to his latter-day Take That nickname of 'The Body'.

One of the people in Howard's breakdancing circles was Jason Orange, the older of twins by twenty minutes, born on 10 July 1970. He came from a similarly big family: as well as Jason's twin Justin there were four other brothers (Simon, Dominic, Samuel and Oliver) with his (now divorced) parents, bus driver Anthony and doctor's PA Jennifer, bringing the family total to seven. Jason is reputed to have blue blood in his veins – family trees suggest he is a direct descendant of King William of Orange, a Dutch Royal plagued by ill health who sat on the British throne as King William III in the second half of the seventeenth century.

'JASON IS REPUTED TO HAVE BLUE BLOOD IN HIS VEINS.'

The Orange family were Mormons, a faith shared by other pop stars including The Mission's bacchanalian front man Wayne Hussey and The Killers' Brandon Flowers. Like Flowers (and very much unlike the rock-and-roll beast that is Wayne Hussey), Jason's family eschewed caffeine and alcohol as drugs and lived very clean lives, something which Jason was able to continue even under the extreme pressures of being in a world-famous boy band.

Like Howard, Jason was not academia's biggest fan. Attending at first Havely Hey School in Whythenshawe until he was 12, and then South Manchester High School, Jason was a keen sportsman, being particularly proficient at swimming, running and football. He has said that he was a quiet pupil and kept himself to himself, so it was perhaps not surprising that when he reached 16 he chose to leave school with only a modest amount of exam passes. On his final day at school he walked through the gates for the last time, turned around, surveyed the buildings where he'd spent so many years and shouted 'Freedom!' out loud. He was keen to work and also joined the infamous Youth Training Scheme, which placed him as a painter and decorator for the Direct Works department of the local council (likewise his twin Justin). Typically, this involved decorating council property and amenities buildings.

It was hardly the most glamorous of work, and although Jason enjoyed it for the four years he was on an apprenticeship there he had his sights set on greater things. In his first teenage year, Jason had also become fascinated with breakdancing – after a brief dalliance with Pink Floyd, whose *The Wall* was the first album he ever bought – so that by his late-teens every spare minute outside of work was spent practising, performing in the streets and watching American videos of the big-name dancers. He joined a local crew called Street Machine that was effectively a rival to Howard Donald's RDS Royals. He too started working the clubs, and this was how he first met Howard at the Apollo. With so much in common they were bound to spark off each other, and a tight dancing partnership was soon formed by the name of Street Beat, which proved to be increasingly lucrative. They could soon command a week's YTS money for one night's work.

Progress was swift for both dancers, who started to rack up television work as well as regular jobs on the club circuit. Jason performed regularly on the TV show *The Hit Man and Her*, presented by Pete Waterman and Michaela Strachan. He'd got the gig after his girlfriend had written to the show telling them of his talent (along with his friend Neil McCartney). Howard, meanwhile, had the technically more impressive but rather less street-credible accolade of performing on that mainstay of conservative TV

schedules *Come Dancing*, during sections of the show dedicated to modern dance.

Realizing their dancing was proving very popular and that there might be a good long-term living to be had beyond the nine-to-five they were used to, Howard and Jason paid a visit to a local music impresario by the name of Nigel Martin-Smith. Unbeknown to them, their lives would never be the same again.

Hailing from the far-from-rock-and-roll town of Oldham in Greater Manchester, Mark Owen was the first future Take That member that Gary Barlow would come into contact with. The product of a northern Catholic family, Mark was born on 24 January 1972 (sharing his birthday with Neil Diamond) and grew up with his brother Daniel and sister Tracey in a modest council house, sharing a room with them for much of his childhood. Such small red-brick terraces were archetypal Mancunian accommodation, made famous by the opening credits of *Coronation Street* (which were actually shot in nearby Salford).

Mark's parents, Keith and Mary, first sent him to be educated at the Holy Rosary Junior School. Mark was a good sportsman, being particularly adept at football despite his relatively diminutive frame, standing at just 5 foot 7 inches tall. One local team he joined, Freehold Athletic, voted him 'Players' Player of the Year' several times, including one season where he scored a hat-trick in a cup final. ('That day will stay with me for as long as I live.') Music Industry Five-a-Side football tournaments are testament to the fact that Mark has lost none of his silky skills, nor his quiet, sportsman-like manners.

But his skills were not always so smooth: 'I got told off all the time for playing football in the house. I broke two windows in one day once. Just as they were fixing the one at the front of the house, I broke the one at the back of the house!' When he broke a window another time, he went and bought a pane of glass to carry out a hasty repair. Unfortunately, his glazing skills weren't quite up to his football ones and his parents came home to find his hands cut to ribbons because of his well-intended but ultimately doomed attempts to repair the window.

His interest in music was developed at an early age, the first record he ever owned being the theme tune to the blockbuster movie *E.T. The Extra Terrestrial*. Unlike Jason and

Howard, however, Mark's general musical taste was somewhat older, with his mother's idol Elvis Presley being a firm favourite. Along with his sister Tracey, he would often dress up as Elvis, complete with blue suede shoes, and entertain people in the alleyway behind his terraced home. (He is still famed for his impersonation of The King, drawn from years of listening to his mum's vast vinyl collection of Presley releases.) This very same alleyway would later become a shrine for Take That fans, who scribble messages of love and support on the wall to this day *à la* Abbey Road, despite Mark's parents not having lived there for many years. Supposedly, his embarrassed mum used to regularly try to bleach the fan graffiti off the wall so as not to annoy her neighbours, and eventually had to post a notice on her front door asking fans not to knock on it all the time.

'UNBEKNOWN TO THEM, THEIR LIVES WOULD NEVER BE THE SAME AGAIN.'

Throughout his time in Take That, Mark has been renowned as famously amiable, laid back and well liked by everyone he works with on a professional level. The media have made no secret that they hold great admiration for him and at any press conference he will always hold court with his self-deprecation and northern humour. Signs of this mellow personality were there at a very young age, and his parents speak of few rows between him and his siblings and friends.

His secondary education started aged 11 at St Augustine's Catholic School, where he would eventually achieve six GCSEs in art, English, maths, religious education, physics and economics (although he failed German, achieving an impressive 13 per cent on one language paper). While his sister Tracey had an excellent voice, Mark developed a love of acting and was a regular in the school drama productions, including the part of Jesus in one Christmas show. Unfortunately his voice started to break mid-scene, as he said in Rick Sky's *The Take That Fact File*: 'Everyone was going around taking the mickey out of me because my speeches were turning into high-pitched squeals. It was so embarrassing.'

The extent of Mark's childhood capers is pretty normal stuff – he and some friends briefly went missing on a school trip to Tenby before finally turning up in a local night-club, having persuaded the bouncers to let them in despite their age. Interestingly, his teachers do not recall Mark being particularly involved with or interested in music when he was at school … it was all about football. He styled himself on former greats such as the late George Best, with his flowing locks and immaculate kit being as much a part of his appearance as the match itself.

By now, Mark's football skills had attracted the interest of several professional teams, not least Manchester United, as well as Huddersfield Town and Rochdale, but a severe groin injury curtailed what had been a promising soccer career. (Being only three years older than David Beckham and also a midfielder, it would have made an enticing team sheet at Old Trafford.) At the time, he was devastated, as soccer had been his main ambition in life. But, like former promising player Gordon Ramsay before him, football's loss was certainly another profession's gain. Years later, on tour with Take That, Mark would always take a football to play with inside the cavernous venues, hotel rooms or studios, earning him the nickname 'Booter'.

As with much of the band, Mark left school aged 16 and got a job, initially in a fashionable clothes shop called Zuttis, then for some time as an electrician's mate, before moving up the career ladder to Barclays Bank in Oldham. The owner of Zuttis, Maggie Hughes, told Rick Sky that he not only impressed her but quite a few girls too: 'He just wanted to earn some money and was really nice, with a big, beaming, bubbling smile on his face.' Despite his apparently meek demeanour, Maggie says Mark was a natural salesman because of the warmth of his personality. (Later, Zuttis would make one of Mark's first ever pair of stage trousers, a see-through nylon number). The Barclays position was destined to last only eight weeks, as another part-time job was about to introduce him to a new friend who would help alter his life forever.

Eager to work, before his final exams Mark had also taken a job as a tea-boy and office hand at the local Strawberry Studios on weekends (his sister Tracey was already working part-time there).

'MARK OFTEN WENT TO GARY'S HOUSE TO LISTEN TO HIS SONGS.'

Mark soon befriended a local boy who was there to work on his demos … Gary Barlow. Mark often went to Gary's house to listen to his songs and watch his friend cut and chop ideas onto his four-track Portastudio. Mark himself listened to the Stone Roses and Blur and even sported a suitably Madchester 'curtain' hair cut. It was a natural progression for Mark to start singing on the demos, and before long the duo formed their first band together, using the dubious moniker of The Cutest Rush. The idea was to perform cover versions as well as Gary's own material. The fledgling band never actually gigged, but it did cement the friendship and perfectly prime two members of Take That for their future careers. Meeting with Gary had an indelible effect on Mark, and his ambition shifted from the world of football to that of music.

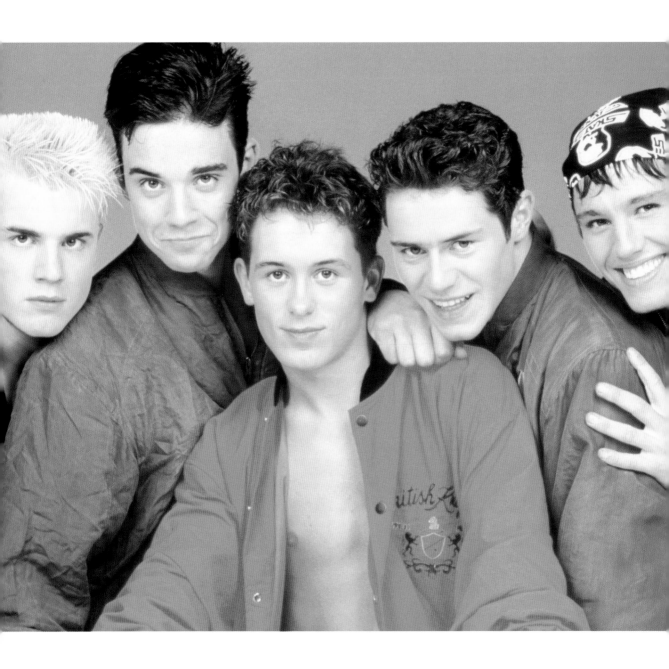

WHO CARES WINS

'SINGERS WANTED: SINGERS AND DANCERS WANTED FOR A NEW BOY BAND. IF YOU HAVE WHAT IT TAKES, CALL NIGEL MARTIN-SMITH AT HIS HALF MOON CHAMBERS OFFICE.'

Actual text of the audition advert for
Take That in the Sun

THERE WERE TWO IMMEDIATE PREDECESSORS to Take That, one British and one American. South London boys Bros were blond near-identical twins playing high-energy, cleverly crafted pop music and selling so many records to teenage girls that legions of so-called Brosettes followed their every move. Lead singer Matt and his drummer twin Luke, as well as their childhood friend Craig on bass, sold millions of records in the late Eighties, changed popular fashions with their Grolsch bottle-top decoration of Dr Martens shoes and generated a hysteria among their fans that many observers likened to Beatlemania – when they did a signing in HMV Oxford Street, 11,000 fans turned up. Songs such as 'When Will I Be Famous?' and 'I Owe You Nothing' shifted hundreds of thousands of copies in a career that included eight Top Ten hits and two No. 1 records.

Just as Bros's reign over the charts was coming to a close, an American group called New Kids on the Block took over the mantle. Already massive in the USA, where they played to football stadiums full of hyperventilating teenage girls, New Kids on the Block invaded the UK's shores in 1989. They were originally conceived as an alternative to New Edition, Bobby Brown's early Jackson Five-inspired group who themselves had enjoyed a hit in 1983 with 'Candy Girl'. Blending the vocal talents and personalities of Donnie Wahlberg, Jordan Knight, Jon Knight, Danny Wood and Joe McIntyre was a masterstroke for New Edition producer Maurice Starr. Five was a magic number – it had worked for the Jacksons, the Osmonds, New Edition and now New Kids on the Block.

Joe McIntyre was only 14 years old on their 1986 début, but within a year of 1988's album *Hangin' Tough* they were the biggest act in America. They cracked Britain too. Between 'You Got It (The Right Stuff)' in 1989 and 'If You Go Away' in 1991, New Kids on the Block scored eleven Top Twenty hits in Britain. Private jets, mansions, fast cars, all the signs of multi-million-dollar success abounded. Hysteria was the air their fans breathed. A management team who could market this new phenomenon properly had a licence to print money.

Nigel Martin-Smith was still a young entrepreneurial businessman watching all of these chart developments with great interest. His Manchester-based modelling agency was very successful and he was well known in North West entertainment circles. However, he had designs on a much grander scale. His idea would turn him into one of the most famous pop managers of all time.

Pop legend has it that Nigel had followed New Kids on the Block's career closely, but when he actually saw them in person at a TV studio in Manchester he was of the

opinion that they were rude and arrogant. Noticing that their behaviour had absolutely no effect on their popularity, he'd thought to himself how massive a boy band could be if they were polite, professional and nice to deal with. He was also keen to recruit his new band from the North, rather than London as was often the norm for pop bands.

Fermenting this idea in his mind, Nigel then had that fateful meeting with Gary Barlow and played the demo tape the young songwriter had given him. Suddenly, almost out of nowhere, Nigel had the centrepiece of his concept: a young, experienced, gifted and very hard-working singer-songwriter. All he needed now was a band to mould around him. Speaking on the TV documentary, *Take That: Where Did It All Go Right?*, he said he was looking for 'metrosexual, northern lads with personality and charisma'.

Gary said he had a friend by the name of Mark Owen who was a good singer and great personality, so Nigel met up with him and immediately saw the potential. Nigel attended an actors' workshop and noticed that whenever Mark got up to speak 'all the girls were grinning'. The jigsaw was coming together nicely. Then, on that day in late 1989 when Jason Orange and Howard Donald walked into Nigel's offices looking for help booking dance work, Nigel knew immediately that his band was quickly gelling around him. He'd seen Jason Orange on *The Hit Man and Her* and after meeting Howard was impressed by both their dancing skills; however, rather than offer them agency services or management guidance as a dance duo, as they had hoped, he surprised them both by suggesting they enrol in a boy band he was putting together. Jason was very reluctant and at first shunned the idea. Admirably, he spoke with his personnel manager at the council about his concerns over the showbiz proposal. Howard was keen from the start and needed no enticing. Eventually, Jason was persuaded by Nigel to meet up with Mark and Gary, whereupon the foursome got on famously and the nucleus of Take That was forged (a nucleus that sixteen years later would become perceived as the 'real' Take That by fans less enamoured with a solo Robbie Williams).

Given Take That's relationship with, and profile in, the British tabloids, it seems only fitting that the elusive fifth member that was to complete the band's line-up came to them through an advertisement in the *Sun*. His name was Robert Peter Williams and his mum went with him to the audition. This green-eyed Stoke-on-Trent boy would go on to become the biggest male solo star of the Nineties and the new millennium, but for now he was literally just an exuberant, hopeful kid turning up for an audition. Entertainment was in his blood: his mum was a singer and his father, Peter Conway, had been a highly regarded comedian who appeared on the TV talent show *New Faces* in the same year that Robbie was born (13 February 1974). Later regarded as Take That's joker, Robbie admits that his first ever record was Alexie Sayle's 'Ullo John Got a New Motor?'. Typically, Robbie has the most glamorous of stars to share his birthday with, including Oliver Reed, George Segal and Peter Gabriel.

In light of his later battles with alcohol, it seems sadly incongruous that Robbie's earliest years were spent growing up in a pub, the Red Lion, which his parents ran.

His now famous obsession with Port Vale Football Club was perhaps inevitable, considering his parents' drinking hole was right next to the club's grounds. (On one match day he showered the passing crowds with his mum's undies.) Sadly, his mum and dad separated when he was only 3 years old, and he moved with his mother Jan and sister Sally to Stoke. 'It didn't have any effect on me,' he later said, 'because I've always been loopy!'

Robbie has a famously close relationship with his mother, and freely admits that during his darkest days to come she was his rock. Back then, Jan ran a ladies' clothes shop, then a small café/bistro and also a florist. Robbie went to Mill Hill Primary School in Tunstall, near Stoke, and then St Margaret's Ward School. He was, perhaps predictably, the class prankster. Former school teachers who have been interviewed by the tabloids confirm this.

Like Mark and Jason, Robbie was a keen sportsman – again, Music Industry Five-a-Side tournaments play testament to his footy skills. Not surprisingly, his extrovert personality was drawn at an early age towards acting as a future profession (he told his mum he had no interest in being a pop star). In his early teens he joined the Stoke-on-Trent Theatre Company, playing small parts in *Pickwick*, *Oliver* (as the Artful Dodger) and *Fiddler on the Roof*. Although he would later claim to struggle with Take That's dance routines, Robbie was also a keen breakdancer.

Robbie left school aged 16 and, after briefly working at his mum's florist's, he took a job as a double-glazing salesman. He was not very good. 'I just used to tell people they were over-priced and leave.' Consequently, this career didn't last long – he quit in order to focus on auditioning for acting roles. Despite his youth, however, he found that most roles were going to even younger actors with experience and often stage-school backgrounds. He did manage to win one role – and a clip that has surfaced on countless *Before They Were Famous* TV shows – is a bit part in the Liverpudlian soap *Brookside*. Years later he had a walk-on cameo role in *EastEnders* (on the phone behind David Wicks), which sounds like the CV of a typical wannabe actor … except that in between these two soap appearances Robbie Williams was in one of the world's biggest boy bands and went on to become the UK's leading solo artist.

The audition for Take That itself was at Nigel's studio, and a nervous Robbie was keen to appear streetwise when he met what might be his future band-mates. 'I came with my mum and I was saying through the corner of my mouth, "Right, Mum, go now."' He walked into the audition and Gary Barlow was sitting in the corner with a leather briefcase full of song sheets, wearing Adidas tracksuit bottoms, Converse trainers, an Italia 90 top and a coiffured Morrissey haircut. Robbie later said he was told, 'This is Gary Barlow, he's a professional club singer and he's going to make this group happen.' Despite thinking at the time that Gary's haircut was ridiculous, Robbie has since admitted that he now sports a similar barnet. Music mythology has it that Gary introduced himself to Robbie and called him 'son'. Gary's confidence was understandable, as Nigel Martin-Smith obviously saw him as the core of the band – after all, by the time of these auditions Gary had composed over fifty songs. Nigel has recalled that Robbie's mum gave him a letter explaining about her son's tap-dancing skills, and the manager remembers how the 16-year-old had 'bags of charisma, with success written all over him'.

Howard had to take a half-day off his job as a vehicle painter to attend the audition, and he was late. When he got there, he asked Nigel, 'Do you think I'll ever earn enough to afford a Toyota Land Cruiser?' to which Nigel replied, 'Yeah, you will.' Robbie said, 'Jason was very confident and liked Ford Escort RS2000 cars, Howard was shy, Mark was great and Gary was the obvious main musical driving force.' Robbie sang 'Nothing Can Divide Us' by teen heart-throb Jason Donovan, but oddly admits, 'I remember thinking what a weird bunch of lads they were and I really didn't think we could ever be a band.'

The audition was soon over and Robbie was told that Nigel would be in touch (afterwards, the boys all went to British Home Stores for some lunch). A few weeks later, Robbie's GCSE results were delivered and he'd failed all but two of them – consistent if nothing else (he got 'shit-faced on Guinness' when he received his results). The very same day, the phone rang and it was Nigel calling with the news that he wanted Robbie in the band. The timing could not have been more serendipitous. In a show of exuberance for which he would later become notorious, Robbie sprinted upstairs into his bedroom, flung the window open and screamed, 'I'm going to be famous!' into the street (pre-empting the notorious exclamation, 'I'm rich! I'm rich beyond my wildest dreams' that a solo Robbie uttered when he signed to EMI in 2002 for £80 million). Back in 1989 Robbie was not yet old enough to drive, and even the eldest, Howard, was only 21. Unbeknown to them, within eighteen months they would not be able to walk down any street in Great Britain without being recognized.

One footnote to add to the embryonic days of Take That is the fact that Nigel Martin-Smith insisted each member brought at least one parent with them to sign his managerial contracts. Pop music is littered with tales of teenage starlets signing contracts that are little more than slave labour. Nigel was clever – he knew that if his master plan with Take That worked, huge sums of money would be generated, and he was adamant that every detail was precise. Being contractually transparent was an admirable first move. Plus, it gained the trust of the boys' parents.

From day one, Nigel's intellect and ideas were absolutely crucial to the band succeeding. This was immediately obvious by the intense programme of rehearsals he arranged, which saw his new charges spending hours every day in dance and choreography sessions, from the early hours until at least 7 p.m. Gary was writing constantly and their voices were improving all the time. Nigel oversaw every aspect of their prospective career, planning it all in intimate detail. The boys were also put on fitness regimes, with sit-ups, press-ups, aerobic work and gymnastics giving the whole experience a real boot-camp atmosphere. Outsiders sometimes wonder why this is so necessary, but if you were to take a bunch of 16- to 20-year-old men and ask them to create a business turning over an eight-figure sum in two years, you would expect there to be some long hours involved.

'THIS IS GARY BARLOW, HE'S A PROFESSIONAL CLUB SINGER AND HE'S GOING TO MAKE THIS GROUP HAPPEN.'

Let's be honest, Take That is a pretty dreadful band name. It's not as bad as The Backstreet Boys and not as good as Foreheads in a Fishtank, but it isn't great. The boys had seen a photograph of Madonna with the caption 'Take That!' written under it and this was elongated to read Take That and Party. The latter two words were dropped when it transpired there already existed an American group called The Party, so that was that … Take That!

When they first heard there was a band called Take That, many music journalists thought it was a joke. It just sounded so limp, so wet. But their success became so huge that people soon forgot the actual words: they became more of a sound that you associated with the five superstars, and any reservations about the moniker completely dissipated.

Over the twelve months after the five members of Take That had each inked the contract with Nigel Martin-Smith, they were still rehearsing and preparing. Rick Sky quoted Gary describing the band's first ever gig in Flicks nightclub in Huddersfield thus: 'There were about twenty people in the audience and a dog. Only about ten of them were watching … but it wouldn't have mattered if only the dog was watching. Afterwards we were on such a high.' That's all those years playing to the pie-and-mash circuit coming in handy right there.

They had finally started to gig, and their workload was exhausting. In the year or so before they hit the big time, Take That took to the road relentlessly, racking up dozens and dozens of shows. At this stage the band's lifestyle was far from glamorous: their average week comprised of piling into Nigel's Ford Escort XR3i and/or a yellow Salford Van Hire vehicle and driving hundreds of miles to play countless gay clubs, then later schools and nightclubs. Funds were understandably tight, so the best they could afford each night was either numerous Little Britain-esque bed and breakfast guest-houses or a long drive home through the small hours. Howard later recalled in ITV1's 2005 documentary, *Take That – For the Record* how most of the gay clubs saw them 'having our arses pinched and our front bits pinched'. If a gig was particularly hostile, 'missiles would be thrown. Some of the audiences were kind enough to give us free beer. Say no more,' said Mark on one occasion. Jason later admitted that he left Take That for about two days during this very early phase, and actually considered going back to painting and decorating – he found the pressures and workload a culture shock but was soon able to gain some perspective and rejoin.

No record companies had shown any interest at this stage, so Take That's début single, 'Do What You Like', was recorded ready for release on Nigel's own Dance UK label in July 1991. Written by Gary with Ray Hedges, who went on to work with Boyzone, the track itself is pretty unforgettable (but for mainly the wrong reasons), a high-energy, keyboard-driven pop song that had none of the sophistication of the band's latter-day pop classics. But this was a band learning as they went along, and the single was sufficiently rousing to help them book yet more live shows to promote it.

In the weeks and months leading up to their début single, the band played scores of gigs. All the time, Nigel Martin-Smith continued working hard to break the band. He arranged press showcases, such as one at Hollywood nightclub in Romford, and spent countless hours on the phone soliciting interest.

Without doubt, the most memorable moment of this fledgling phase of Take That was the bizarre and risqué promo video they shot for 'Do What You Like', which would make The Village People blush. It was shot for a modest budget of only £5,000 in Stockport, which is not currently famed for its glitzy showbiz vistas. In a blatant attempt to capture the pink pound, the boys were filmed in a white-wall studio wearing virtually nothing but numerous leather jockstrap-style combinations, codpieces and studded leather. Copious amounts of jelly were slapped and rubbed over various naked body parts and there was enough cavorting aplenty to make Will Young look like Arnold Schwarzenegger. Gary Barlow's hair was a miracle of modern science, and the only thing tighter than the jockstraps was the budget. According to legend, the closing bum shot was so hotly sought after that the boys each auditioned – a screen-test for arses, believe it or not – to see whose was better. Not surprisingly, the moral minority complained the clip was too obscene and pornographic, but the vast majority took it as intended – a tongue-in-cheek bit of fun. Nonetheless, even David Brent from

The Office would cringe watching the blatantly homoerotic video. It was all a far cry from seeing a velvet-voiced Robbie play the Royal Albert Hall years later in a suave lounge suit, but this was their first foray into the pop world and it is rare that a pop band nails their image from day one.

It is odd looking back at this video and the early photographs of Take That, because, to be honest, their look is laughable. Leather gear, tassels and tight trousers: it was all so camp and exaggerated. Fast-forward to the sophisticated, grainy images of 'Patience' and it might as well be a different band. But some context is needed. This was a bunch of young guys who – with the exception of Gary Barlow – had relatively

little entertainment experience. Contrary to popular belief, they were involved in their own look to some degree – they would shop in High Street Kensington at places such as Hyper Hyper, the amazing alternative clothes emporium where young, break-through designers often sold their wares direct.

This look would quickly subside as Nigel began to notice a strange thing happening at a lot of their club shows – specifically, one night when they played an under-age mixed-sex club in Hull. Nigel – ever perceptive – noticed that the reaction to his band from the girls was actually far more frantic than from the gay clubs they'd been focusing on. Cleverly re-focusing his strategy, Nigel twigged immediately that he had a boy-band sensation in the making, and he began to book scores of mixed-sex nightclubs in order to confirm his suspicions.

At this point, Take That was just another pop band in among the thousands of wannabes trying to make it. But Nigel was more than just your average pop-band manager. Somehow, he got them a slot on a satellite TV show called *Cool Cube*. Gary worked on new material especially for the performance, including a track called 'Waiting Around', and they prepared special dance routines too. The tight hot pants they wore might have been better suited to a soft-porn channel but the viewers (perhaps because of, rather than despite, the shorts) approved and the band were asked back several times. Breaking a pop band on TV is a crucial way of operating in the modern climate and Nigel was ahead of his time in using that medium to gain exposure (in more ways than one) for his band (especially important because Simon Bates was the lone DJ playing their music on Radio 1 with any frequency). Furthermore, Nigel under-

stood the need to have omnipresent press coverage, and managed to get a press officer called Carolyn Norman to work for the band before they had even had a hit, and was pivotal in orchestrating the band's amazing press profile right from the early days. Thus, as quickly as June 1991, she had managed to shoe-horn the band coverage in various teen magazines such as *My Guy*, *Jackie*, *Number 1* and *Smash Hits*.

The infamous jelly-smearing video was first shown in July 1991 on another influential TV show, Pete Waterman's *The Hitman and Her*, the very same show that Jason had previously appeared on as a dancer.

This coincided with the release date of their début single, entirely self-financed by Nigel and his partner – a real risk for them, and also a genuine show of faith in the band's potential. Nigel had already spent close to £100,000 investing in Take That.

'Do What You Like' charted at No. 82.

THE FUSES ARE LIT

THE FURORE SURROUNDING THE RAUNCHY video may not have helped the début single chart but it did contribute to seducing the major record label RCA to sign the band in September 1991. At the time, RCA's head of A&R was Korda Marshall, who would later go on to found his own record label and sign Muse, Ash, Garbage and The Darkness before a highly successful stint as the Managing Director of Warner Brothers Records UK, but in the early days his experience with Take That had a pivotal impact, both good and bad, on Korda's own career.

> 'IT'S EASY TO SEE HOW HE PERSUADED RCA
> TO COMMIT TO A BAND THAT NO OTHER
> LABEL WAS INTERESTED IN.'

'The irony was,' Korda told me for this book, 'that when we finally signed them to RCA it was actually the third time we'd looked at them. Originally one of our scouts brought them in but we were not convinced about all the leather-bondage imagery and suchlike; the second time, a guy called David Donald brought it to an A&R meeting but again we did not commit; then the third time one of our senior A&R managers called Nick Raymonde brought a Take That demo into a meeting, just a few months after he'd joined the company. It was a three-track demo with "Take That and Party", "Million Love Songs" and "Do What You Like".'

Before now, Nick Raymonde has never been interviewed at length about his time with Take That – he worked with them on a daily basis for the entire length of their 'first' career (as against since they re-formed) and, as the key A&R man, was their central contact with the record company. Talking to the author exclusively for this book, Raymonde still speaks about the band with real passion and it is easy to see how he persuaded RCA to commit to a band that no other label was interested in:

'I'd been doing club promotion for ten years before I started work at RCA, promoting dance music predominantly. I had started looking through all the pop magazines that I hadn't really looked at for years, doing mental research – suddenly I'm reading

all these magazines that I'd never looked at before like *Smash Hits*, *Number 1*, *Just Seventeen* and so on.

'So I'd been reading through all this pop press and, in the back of my mind, the idea started to ferment that there weren't any new pop stars – they were all TV stars: Jason and Kylie, *Beverley Hills 90210*, etc. I didn't think, "Right, I'll go out and sign a pop group," it was just registered in my mind. Then a scout called Dave Donald brought in this video of some TV Take That had done and said, "You've got to see this video, it's hilarious." I watched the video and I didn't think it was hilarious, I thought it might be an opportunity.

'The lads were sort of boy-next-door, just dead ordinary, and they gave off the vibe that they were really enjoying what they were doing. I contacted Nigel and it turned out they'd been turned away by RCA – they ended up sitting down in reception and not even being seen – so he was quite amused by the whole situation. By this time he'd been rejected by so many people he'd actually raised £50,000 to make the infamous "Do What You Like" video – he spent even more of his own money on school shows. He just thought, "Fuck it, I'm going to do it myself," which is amazing really. Him being involved was a big plus: I liked Nigel, he was one of those few people in the record industry like Tom Watkins, Jazz Summers and Malcolm McLaren – real larger-than-life characters. People don't always realize but he is hysterically funny, he has you in stitches, yet at the same time he is totally driven.

'I went to see them do a PA [Personal Appearance] at an under-18s club in Slough at four o'clock one afternoon. They were supporting Right Said Fred, who were just about to have a big hit with "I'm Too Sexy". They were sat in the dressing room and I went and said hello and they were all dressed in this ridiculous bondage gear, but it was entertaining! Once they went on stage there was sort of thirty or forty girls stood around the fringes, pretty disinterested in what was happening on stage and more interested in the boys that were there to chat them up. And do you know what? By the time Take That had finished doing the first song, they were completely mobbed. As I said, I'd done club promotion for so long, so I just did some simple multiplication: there's about 4,500 clubs in the UK and of that I reckoned there were probably 1,000 of them that you could put this band on at; therefore, if you get the same reaction at

each club, then make a decent record and somehow aggregate all the fans together, then you could be successful.

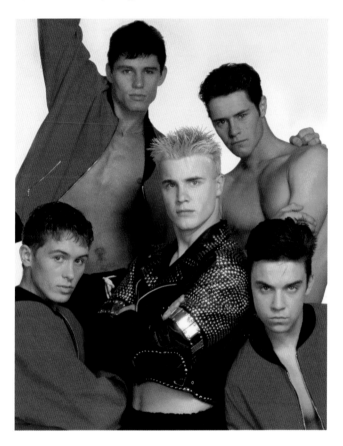

'Because they weren't on the radar yet, I thought we could have a clear run at them as a project – Korda was a hugely experienced A&R guy and I thought that he would help me with it. He wanted me to succeed because he'd actually brought me into the record label as the A&R manager, so he wanted me to be successful.'

So Nick took the tracks, to his boss and this time Korda was hooked by one track in particular: 'I remember listening to "A Million Love Songs" and thinking *That's a smash record,*' says Korda. Nigel Martin-Smith had a very clear vision of what to do and I thought Gary's songs were really very good. '"A Million Love Songs" had that sax solo, there was something going on in there from chord progressions to harmony, melody, the whole feel. Yet what people won't realize is that Take That were actually a bit of a joke at the time in the A&R community, and in fact when Nick brought the tape into that meeting, everybody kind of laughed. But Nick took it seriously.'

Nick agrees: 'As we were going through the process of signing the band, everyone is telling me that I'm an idiot. "This is going to be your first signing for RCA, Nick, and you're gonna sign this joke group that everyone has turned down!" Hearing all this, I started to get cold feet; I started to imagine how it would look if it all failed, the losses we'd make and so on. I mentioned this to Korda and he said a remarkable thing: "Look, if you sign them and they are successful, you're a star and we're all laughing because they'll sell millions of records; and if they fail, you can blame me." It was amazing. No one has ever brought that to light, Korda's never mentioned that and it was unheard of for someone to put it like that. So we decided we'd sign them.'

The context for this relative scorn was that, for many, pop was dead. As mentioned earlier, Bros had ruled the pop world in the late Eighties and New Kids on the Block had taken over their crown shortly after, but since then many ears had either turned to the Pacific West Seaboard and the approaching juggernaut that was grunge, or lost a few brain cells in the rush for ecstasy and raving. Guitars and clubbing were back in, and a squeaky-clean boy band with carefully choreographed dance routines was in many ways the absolute anti-thesis of what was considered fashionable.

'YOU LOOK FOR A GAP. THAT'S WHAT WE SAW WITH TAKE THAT.'

'I remember the day we signed them,' Korda told the author. 'We got all these faxes from Sony and EMI basically saying, "What the fuck are you doing? You're the laughing stock of the A&R community!" But you have to look at it from a social and cultural aspect, about whether there is a space with nobody in it. For example, years later I went to see Deep Purple and Lynyrd Skynyrd and you could see there was a huge audience for that style of music but there was nobody new doing it … and then I came across this band called The Darkness. Likewise, there was a phase in the early 2000s where there weren't a lot of singer-songwriters around; there were a few "arty farty" singers and some quality people like Damien Rice, but for me there was no mainstream commercial singer-songwriter. Then I heard James Blunt. You look for a gap. That's what we saw with Take That.'

Nick Raymonde and Korda both spotted this vacuum. 'There were no boy bands, nobody was doing pop in that sense. It was the whole club/dance thing. Nick and I went to see Take That at a club called the Limelight in Shaftesbury Avenue where they did a three-song set which, to be honest, was so gay it was funny. They were still quite young at the time. They could obviously dance, the routines were fantastic, and I recall being struck by their complexions. It sounds funny but they were obviously going to be very photogenic. I could just see them all over magazines such as *Smash Hits*. If you look at any early photos, you have to agree there was a clear photogenic sensibility. I know this sounds silly, but even something as specific as their individual jaw lines, the way that their skin looked – Nigel Martin-Smith had done a good job of styling them too by then.

'That night I remember thinking they could all dance really well, they'd got a good mix of looks and personalities, and they'd got a couple of songs that could be hits … Let's go for it! That impulse was actually so unlike me. Normally I'd strategize and make a decision on the music and the core creativity and suchlike.

'As I say, in the very early days it was very gay. It was Nigel Martin-Smith who put it together and it was a market he thought they could tap into. When he came in, we had a long conversation about trout fishing, which I love – he's a fisherman as well, so we talked about trout for most of the time. I got on with him really well. He had his own model agency in Manchester at the time, yet for this new boy band he had a really strong vision about what he wanted to do. This was crucial in the decision-making process, because it was evident that it wasn't just five young boys new to the business, which has the potential to be a nightmare. I was effectively dealing with one grown-up man who knew exactly what he was doing.

'I'd met the actual band on the night of the Limelight gig, and then they came into the office and we chatted and talked. It was really evident that they were really good at gripping-and-grinning [meeting and greeting the general public], which, in a pop sense, is really important. At the Limelight and in our offices you could watch them working a room, chatting with women; they were great with women and they were really good with the media and they'd shake hands, they'd be interested and they'd turn up on time. I know it sounds silly but the ability for them to turn up at a TV studio at half six in the morning, looking bright, fresh, ready to go and cracking jokes when everyone else is blotchy-eyed, it was a hefty potential asset … in walk these five young kids and you couldn't not look at them. You could see them being so attractive to women, which is an obvious bonus. Plus they were really respectful with their p's and q's. They were nice kids, well brought up, good characters. And, contrary to many reports, at that point they were certainly a gang, the five of them were together all that time, laughing constantly, mucking about. It was all new and fresh. They were a gang.

'At this point we started to take them seriously. Nigel took us seriously, and we finally agreed a record contract – it wasn't a huge deal at all. It was in the region of about £70,000, which effectively committed RCA to a further investment of around £300,000 to £400,000 in terms of launching Take That. It was a pretty standard deal to be honest.'

Nigel and the boys' hard work had finally paid off and they had secured themselves a major-label record contract. Take That joined a very unique roster that boasted such diverse artists as Rick Astley, The Primitives, The Wedding Present and Pop Will Eat Itself. 'I actually had several occasions where the paths of these polar opposites on our roster would cross,' Korda told me. 'High-profile new bands are usually signed in something of a fanfare, to start the PR machine rolling early. I remember the signing party for Take That very clearly. It was at the Hard Rock Café. We all had a long chat and I started talking to Robbie. The rest of the band were all drinking Coca Cola and Robbie was like, "Can you shove a scotch in there, please?" We had to look around to see where his manager and everyone else was before we gave him this sneaky drink. Bless them, they were under the thumb of Nigel in quite a big way, but in a positive sense; Nigel did a lot of good things for them and that was because he was very strong in knowing what he wanted to do and where he wanted to take it. He controlled the

boys and I think their frustrations would later come through, but from a record label's perspective Nigel's approach was a very positive aspect, because there was someone in charge, sailing the ship and knowing what to do.'

Take That's first major-label single was 'Promises' in September 1991, exactly seven days before Nirvana's seminal 'Smells Like Teen Spirit'. One record changed the face of modern music, arts, TV, radio, music-industry strategies and pretty much every facet of popular culture; the other one didn't. No prizes for guessing which one was Take That's.

Nick Raymonde recalls that first major-label release: 'I thought Gary was a great song-writer, but being honest, "Promises" was an all right song, but it wasn't a great record. On top of that, we hadn't worked out how to get all of these fans that existed everywhere alerted to the fact a record was coming out. There was so much hype around the group that the record company was almost wanting it to succeed too soon. This song was done with Duncan Bridgman at his own studio in Uxbridge Road: he produced it, played on it, but unfortunately I didn't like it – to be fair to Duncan, though, I didn't really know what record it was we were trying to make.'

Having said that, the single did mark the start of something big, not least their first ever chart entry. Robbie later remarked that the moment they all heard the single had charted at No. 38 – their first chart hit – was the most excited he has ever been about any single, including during his own illustrious solo career. Apparently, the band jumped on his hotel bed so much it broke.

Nick Raymonde was equally pleased. 'I thought when that first record had gone in at No. 38 that was a genuine hit, because at that time the Top Forty was regarded as success – actually, the fact that it only sold about 8,000 copies and probably hadn't even washed its hands on the cost of the photograph on the sleeve was a more worrying reality.'

The video was low budget but did give an interesting insight into the band's life on the road, featuring as it did footage of their club PAs and school shows, as well as a live performance re-enacted at Hollywood nightclub in Romford, one of their regular haunts. During the promotional campaign for 'Promises' they also made their first appearance on *Wogan*, which was Britain's biggest chat show at the time, with viewing figures of 12 million a night. As part of his intro, Sir Terence called them – not for the first or last time – 'Britain's answer to New Kids on the Block'.

'IT WAS ALL NEW AND FRESH. THEY WERE A GANG.'

Nigel Hassler of Helter Skelter Agency was, at the time, working for Primary Talent booking agents, and he became involved in some of Take That's very earliest shows. Even at that early stage there was a growing buzz within the music industry about these newcomers, as he explained to me exclusively for this book:

'I am always researching magazines, gig listings, seeing who keeps cropping up, who I need to keep an eye out for, and Take That seemed to catch my eye every now and then. So I went to the record label and Nick Raymonde put me in contact with Nigel Martin-Smith. The buzz was building already so I phoned him and said I'd love to get involved. I was employed by Nigel Martin-Smith to try to get them on any kind of club show, mainly under-18s discos, the odd gay club and a schools tour. There was a combination of markets there from way back then. Basically, though, at that stage it was like pulling teeth trying to get them booked, and it was always for very low fees. We were

almost giving the band away to give them exposure: I think it was about £200 a night on average.' Given that this money had to cover fuel, food, any accommodation if it was needed and so on, it is easy to see that everyone involved was, at this point, just investing their efforts in the future.

Their innovative manager was very keen to gig the band as hard as possible – at the time this was a relatively forward-thinking strategy, one of hard road-work normally reserved for more rock-oriented acts. 'Everybody was working very hard to break the band,' explains their former agent Nigel Hassler, 'yet it was actually quite difficult to fill up a date sheet; gigs were not easy to come by. Nigel Martin-Smith would take anything, so they ended up travelling all over the country: Ipswich, then up north, then way back south, miles and miles and miles, wherever they could play in front of people.'

Far from concentrating on almost exclusively gay clubs, Nigel Hassler saw a much more focused attention on school tours. 'In my opinion,' continues Hassler, 'it was the first time this school touring schedule had been done so strategically. Occasionally the odd band may have done one or two school shows, but none had actually gone and done a deliberate schools' tour. That's what we were putting together for them. The typical day would involve playing a school in the afternoon, perhaps with a meet-and-greet afterwards and a quick signing session, then off to a club show and very often back in the car for a drive to a late-night club, not always in the same towns. Week-ends were always two shows a night. It was relentless. They really put in the time.'

Having seen literally thousands of gigs in his career, Nigel Hassler was impressed by the band's show even when they were playing tiny venues for next to no money: 'They were great; they looked good, the choreography was fantastic, the costumes were well thought out, they looked like the "real deal". You often get rock bands who can't perform too well and they need a couple of years to actually develop and grow to become an accomplished live band, but from what I remember, Take That were doing very well indeed so early on. I actually went to one of their earliest London shows at the Brixton Fridge for a gay club night. They would usually play about five songs, playback with a live vocal. They were very, very good.'

Despite the paltry financial returns, Nigel recalls that their record label was firmly behind them: 'BMG were giving them major push-ups to make some connection with the public. We had a few problems with show dates clashing with some booked by Nigel Martin-Smith's office, and when I spoke to him about a few concerns it was taken as me ducking out of doing work on the band; we had a bit of a disagreement and that was the end of the relationship. It was a fairly short affair but very interesting to see Take That at such an early stage in their careers. I think I may have made about five hundred quid out of the band!'

SOMETHING
REMARKABLE THIS
WAY COMES

UNFORTUNATELY, CHART MATTERS WERE ONLY to get worse. In January and February 1992 the band embarked on a gruelling 'Safe Sex' tour of predominantly gay and under-18s clubs – complete with the support of the Family Planning Association – as part of their concerted promotion for the second RCA single, 'Once You've Tasted Love' (Howard has admitted that the contradiction between a Safe Sex tour and the raunchy 'Do What You Like' video did not escape them). More gigs were played – sometimes four a day – radio and TV had started picking up on the boys, and with the might of RCA's press office behind them, all eyes were on a chart position higher than the No. 38 achieved by 'Promises'. The campaign was assisted – sort of – by the promo video, which, although it didn't feature naked arses and bondage gear, still had the boys prancing around in a rehearsal studio, wearing the sort of eye-watering, skin-tight lycra last seen on a Tour de France winner.

In the first week of February, 'Once You've Tasted Love' fell well short of the Top Forty at No. 47. This was an unmitigated disaster. Take That were a band in crisis. The night they found out, they were on the road and all admitted they cried at the news. There was even talk of splitting up if things didn't improve.

For Nick Raymonde at RCA, this was a real shocker: 'I was in a bit of a rarefied balloon because Take That were all over the pop press so you think, *They're huge, I'll put a record out and it'll be massive.* Everyone was hyping everybody. No one wanted to say, "Hold on a minute. Is that record good enough?" I've been there so many times, because you get caught up in the hype and no one says, "We've made a video, we've spent £30,000 making the record, we've given them an advance and it's shit."'

Yet Nick still buoyed spirits and sat them down to pep-talk them. 'The band were grafting their tits off, but when they wandered in after the second single had gone in at No. 47 they looked like beaten men. I said, "Look, we are going to do this, we will win, we just have to get the record company on board and all you've got to do is tour and tour and tour and tour and tour. I have to make you a hit record." And that's exactly what we did.'

'I HAVE TO MAKE YOU A HIT RECORD.'

To compound their problems, the band had started work on their début album and it was proving to be a far from straightforward process. The album sessions had started at Southlands Studios in London over the Christmas period and were riddled with complications. Almost an entire album's worth of tracks had been recorded, but Korda Marshall at RCA wasn't entirely happy with them. Nick Raymonde and Korda knew they weren't getting it quite right, as Nick recalls: 'I listened to the track we had, then sat back with Korda and said, "It's not really any good, is it?" So it wasn't really a great place to be.'

Korda told me about the behind-the-scenes issues: 'At that point I had a band called Londonbeat, a male harmony group, who'd had a couple of big hits, most famously with "I've Been Thinking About You". I had a meeting with a producer called Ian Levine to discuss working on Londonbeat with him. It came up in that conversation about what else I was working on and I explained we were in the middle of making this album with Take That and it wasn't happening at the moment. I said, "We've spent a fortune making this album which just doesn't sound very good, it's too Pet Shop Boys-sounding."'

Ian Levine was a maverick music-industry heavyweight with a portfolio of hits and artists as hefty as RCA's growing Take That overdraft, including work with Erasure, Nina Carroll, The Pasadenas and the Pet Shop Boys (he would later also work with Blue). Ian had been the UK's top club DJ in the Seventies, famed for his profile and reputation in the Northern Soul scene and later as resident DJ at the legendary Heaven nightclub. To date, along with the eighty hits he has produced or remixed, Ian is also listed as one of the Top Ten Most Influential DJs of All Time by Bill Brewster in his book *Last Night a DJ Saved My Life*. For Take That's ambitions of getting their début album right, Ian seemed like he could be a magic bullet.

'So I had this meeting with Korda,' Ian explained to me for this biography. 'I'd been brought in previously to produce The Pasadenas, who looked like they were going to be dropped, and we came up with a hit single – I was told I was being brought in to resurrect their career and yet it actually resurrected my career because I'd had a few years

where things hadn't gone very well and I'd nearly lost my house over one project in particular. So I gave The Pasadenas their biggest hit, "Tribute (Right On)", which was Top
Five for weeks.

'With that in mind, Korda asked me to come in and talk about Londonbeat. Suddenly, in the middle of the conversation we started talking about Take That and he
said, "I'm very frustrated. I've put a lot of money into this band," and Korda was very
unhappy with what had been done.

'I was well aware of Take That because I was in admiration of what their press officer Carolyn Norman had done with them, which was take a group who hadn't made a
hit and somehow plaster them over every single magazine going regardless – everyone
was talking about them. However, the general feeling that I'd heard in the industry
about Take That, the word on the street if you like, was that here was a group surrounded by a lot of hype, a lot of publicity but with crap material. At the end of the
day, no matter how much money you spend on an act, if the songs aren't there you're
not going to make it … and the songs weren't there.'

The band themselves have said they were becoming the most famous group in
Britain for not having a hit. The problem for Korda was that his budgets were already

shot: 'There was no money left to make the album again, so the irony of this story was that we gave Ian Levine a royalty as well as a small fee. Normally he was charging about £15K a song, but because RCA didn't have any spare cash for the projects I agreed to give him a really big royalty. So when Take That went on to sell millions it was a great deal for him. He said to me, "Korda, next time you want something doing, don't pay me any advances, just give me a really big royalty again! That's the best thing you ever made me do."'

Ian had grand dreams for the band but had to be very creative with such a limited budget: 'The most we could squeeze together for recording was twenty grand, with

which I had to cut five tracks, including flying in Billy Griffin [former lead singer with The Miracles] from Los Angeles to get the right sound I wanted for the vocals. I had an expensive studio in Chiswick and I had to use live musicians like a sax player and a guitar player. It was all very expensive. It cost me much more than that twenty grand to make, but I had to make a decision – RCA couldn't come up with any more money and I wanted to do it. Fortunately, in the end I did very well out of it because of my royalty being increased.'

Once the new sessions had been set up, Ian was in his element: 'We went in and the first meeting with the group was down at the studio. Jason wasn't involved in any of the studio recordings but he came down on the first day to meet me, so we had all five of them there. We all went out to a restaurant called New Orleans, one of those Tex-Mex places that do char-coal-grilled hamburgers and food like that. It's even done out like Bourbon Street in New Orleans with big awnings and all that stuff. I remember we went in their car – it was a big, dark blue Previa people-carrier. They had no money for a road manager so Gary had been doing a lot of the driving up and down the country for all these under-18 gigs. I sat in the front seat with Gary. When we had this dinner, they were the nicest guys I'd ever met, and I thought at the time, *If we give them a hit they won't change at all*. They were genuine and humble. Gary and Robbie were saying things like, "Ian, we are really pleased to be working with you, we know what you've done in the past."'

Ian says Take That were pretty typical of a boy band in the studio: 'They all knuckled down eventually, but they'd muck about and were always laughing and joking. Gary was very serious about knuckling down, he was very responsible – when they came back later in the year to redo some stuff, Gary had really got his act together and did loads of backing vocals. I think he's very talented and I liked him very much. Korda thought bringing in a veteran such as Billy Griffin was a great idea: the process wasn't about bringing in someone to sing the songs for them, it was about bringing in a great vocalist from America to help the boys learn about breathing and vocal techniques and add some of the harmonies and melodies, give the BVs [backing vocals] some strength and colour.'

Korda had his own thoughts about where the band's vocals could go: 'Robbie was a cheeky chappy naturally, but there was something about him. He was always one of the strongest voices, and I remember saying to Ian that we shouldn't just focus on Gary, we should try and bring some of the others out. It was evident that Robbie could actually sing. Mark could sing too. They could all sing backing vocals and hold a tune, but they weren't great singers at that point because they hadn't had any experience of learning how to sing properly in a studio. I signed them because they were great dancers, had good complexions and a couple of hit songs and I thought I could work the vocals out.'

While Gary Barlow was the creative hub of Take That, Ian Levine saw something in Robbie that he wanted to explore. 'They were messing around in the studio and I heard Robbie's voice and I said, "Robbie, you should be singing some lead." He just said, "Don't be daft." At that point he saw himself as the clown in the group, just dancing around and mucking about, having fun. I thought his voice was better than Gary's, to be honest.

'They were all very wet behind the ears but Robbie was the most inexperienced. I wanted him to sing lead regardless. He had a fantastic-sounding voice, he just hadn't learned how to sing in the studio. He could sing a song perfectly with no music playing, but when the music came on he couldn't pitch in tune and would end up singing in a different key. But I took a lot of care because I thought he was worth nurturing, I thought he was a raw talent. He was very appreciative of that. Months later we had a press conference for the launch of the album *Take That and Party*, and were upstairs in the private bar. Robbie was quite near me and one of the newspapermen who was in my earshot asked Robbie what made him start singing lead. He put his arm around me and said, "Come here, big fella," then said, "I owe it all to this guy, Ian Levine. He's the one who persuaded me to sing lead." He was actually very acknowledging of the fact publicly to the press in 1992.

'I am proud of picking him out at that raw level when he couldn't even sing in tune – that vindicates certain things to me. Sometimes, if you ever doubt your own abilities, which you do when you have a bad period, things like that help. How many people can do that? It's like picking the *X Factor* winner out of 75,000 people.'

One controversial choice for the album was a cover of the song made famous by Barry Manilow, called 'Could It Be Magic?'. There's a fine balance between the camp chic of Manilow and the undoubted quality and professionalism of his song writing, and covering his music is a high-risk business. Interestingly, though, Ian Levine was coming from an altogether different angle for this idea: 'I'd never heard Barry Manilow's original, I only knew of the 1976 disco version by Donna Summer, which big gay clubs in America treated as an anthem. When I was working at Heaven as a DJ, we would always put that record on at the big party nights. It was revered by everyone, it was a god-like record.'

Nick recalls that Korda recognized that there was a need to have one absolute dead-certain record that was going to nail it. Korda recalls the tension this suggestion created: 'I like to sign an act if they've got the songs. I make a big deal of that. So when I said we are going to do a Barry Manilow cover, some people at RCA looked at me as if to say, "What the fuck are you talking about?"'

'WE WERE CONSTANTLY TRYING TO INVENT NEW WAYS OF PRESENTING THE GROUP.'

'I cut the original Take That version,' explains Ian, 'and the first mix was directly influenced by the Donna Summer arrangement.' With Ian's brilliant high-energy disco-style version on the vinyl album, Nick Raymonde also contacted the Italian producers the Rapino Brothers about remixing a version as a club promo. They had recently done 'Love Me the Right Way' for Kym Mazelle and that had been a big hit.

'What I wanted to do,' Nick told me, 'was bend the perception of Take That a little, from being a pop group into being a band that had maybe something else attached to them. Even later, when they were having hits, still radio wouldn't play them so we had to say, "Look, they're not crap, they're actually quite cool, they've got an Italian hard-core house remix and look at the video, it's quite cool …" We were constantly trying to invent new ways of presenting the group.'

Speaking to me for this book from their Italian studio in early 2006, Charlie of the Rapino Brothers revealed more: 'We were having problems finding the right way forward, we were struggling for about four days. We were always fighting, shouting in Italian, and the band would just sit there on the sofa watching this Italian comedy. Then Marco fell asleep for half an hour and then said, "Let's do it like 'Freedom' by Wham!", so it sounds like that.'

Marco remembers the record label's reaction. 'When we delivered it we were told they said, "I can't believe those two Italian bastards have delivered a worldwide smash!" This track was originally planned as a club promo entitled "The Rapino Brothers featuring Take That" but then it was made into a seven-inch and people loved it.' Charlie says, 'Gary Barlow was on tour when he heard it and he said when he heard the mix he went nuts! This was eventually the version of the song that won the Brits "Best Single" of 1992 with the production credit of the Rapino Brothers/I. Levine/Billy Griffin.' (Oddly, the band was not invited to perform at the ceremony that year, quite a snub given their profile.)

Stephen Budd, who manages the two Italians, remembers those times with relish: 'I got this call from Nigel Martin-Smith and he said, "What have you done? I've got them in the studio with those Italians and they've got soft-core mags! Tell them not to bring those magazines into the studio ever again!" Also, what was amazing was that when they were working with us there were these code words. We were issued a list of code words to tell us which day and which studio they would be at and we were not supposed to talk to each other unless we used these code words – the problem being that if the fans found out about it there'd be two thousand girls outside the studio. Robbie used to go to the Rapinos' house but they were always well behaved in front of Nigel. The only scandals were with the Rapino Brothers themselves.'

Charlie agrees: 'The band turned up with bodyguards at the studio some days when there were no fans around and we were like, "What do you need bodyguards for?" and we later realized it was probably to protect Take That from us!'

Stephen Budd loved the result: 'We were in the Roundhouse for the seven-inch version of "Could It Be Magic?" and Nick Raymonde came in and listened to it and we all had that moment when you know without a shadow of a doubt we had a monster smash record – that very rarely happens, it was a big moment. Nothing was going to stop it being a huge hit, clear as daylight.'

The fans weren't the only ones who loved the song: 'We then took a call from Barry Manilow,' recalls Stephen Budd. 'He said, "I've heard this arrangement and it's the best I have heard of one of my songs that I didn't do, so could you come over and meet us at Wembley Arena?" So we did and met him and he did the actual arrangement live on stage, which was a nice moment.'

The use of two versions of the song did cause controversy behind the scenes, but Ian Levine's scintillating mix was available on the vinyl while the Rapino version was on the CD format. For Take That fans interested in seeing one song treated in equally fascinating ways, both tracks are vital.

As far as the public were concerned, Take That was still a fledgling boy band with only one chart hit to their name and no album to speak of. After the disastrous chart placing for 'Once You've Tasted Love', there was enormous pressure on the next single – the band's fourth. In the post-millennial climate, a boy band with a seven-figure investment behind them would probably not reach their fourth single with statistics as poor as Take That's were at this stage. Korda Marshall and Nick Raymonde's belief in the band remained strong, but the lack of a chart success was heaping pressure on the balance sheets at RCA. Ultimately, it cost Korda his job.

'After those first two RCA singles had stiffed,' says Korda, 'there was a lot of pressure on me because of the lack of success and the un-recouped debit balance that was on my head. If you included the spiralling album costs, RCA had spent a million quid on Take That and they weren't even going in the Top Forty. To make matters worse, I'd also signed a band called M People that had also stiffed at that point. So here I was, I was carrying the can of a million quid on one band and 1.2 million on the other. That's the nature of pop bands, it's like rolling two dice and trying to get a double six. A new MD came in to the company, looked at what was going on and said, "There's nothing really here," so I was dismissed.' The début album was still to be completed at this point.

Less than two months after Korda stopped working at RCA, Take That released their third single on the label, a cover of Tavares' disco classic 'It Only Takes a Minute Girl', which, to everyone's delight, flew into the Top Ten at No. 7 on its June 1992 release, spending a full two months in the lists. The excellent video featured some incredible dancing from Howard and Jason – a frequently missed or underrated aspect of the band's original success.

The record company and band mustered up huge PR opportunities, dozens of signings, meet-and-greets, store appearances, club shows and PAs, everything anyone could think of to work the record. There was also a very clever strategy of data collection, which might sound like some business buffoonery to the average pop fan but was actually a very astute piece of marketing on RCA's part, as Nick Raymonde explains:

'HUGH SUGGESTED THEY ASK FANS TO FILL IN FORMS EACH AND EVERY SINGLE TIME THE BAND PLAYED.'

'I'd got one shot left after the first two singles had stiffed. So I went in to see Hugh Goldsmith [Head of Marketing at RCA], and said, "I need you to come and see Take That. Come with me because it's only if you see them, then do the maths like I did, that you will understand the potential and, hopefully, think of the missing link that will stop the next single failing." We drove up to Warrington to see them at a club PA and he just watched the show, turned to me and said, "Yeah, I get it. I totally understand what we need to do." Hugh suggested they ask fans to fill in forms each and every single time the band played, so that they had the addresses and details of what they knew to be a large fan base. This might be standard procedure now, but back in 1991 it was innovative stuff. And it was all done manually, as e-mail was not yet commonplace. Within five weeks, RCA had over 10,000 girls' names on a list. So when the song was released, the fans knew about it and … bingo.'

The track was recorded with producer Nigel Wright at his home, which had a studio and swimming pool, so it was an enjoyable experience. The choice of song was also a masterstroke, giving the band huge visibility overnight. Given that the previous two singles had only spent five weeks in the charts put together, this was massive progress, but most importantly it put Take That in the Top Ten and onto the nation's television sets. Take That had finally broken through.

Nick recalls how the band's work ethic and personalities proved priceless in those early days when they were up against the odds: 'I was starting to build a loyalty in the record company towards this group – the underdogs, if you like. There were certain people who had seen the band, met them and loved them. They endeared themselves to people. The press officer for RCA was a girl called Loretta and she just fell in love with them; everyone who was working on them absolutely adored them. Nigel was very good with all of this too, and supported all those people, so you suddenly started to get this Take That bubble within RCA, which was quite powerful. That can only help a young band massively and that was down to them being genuinely lovely guys.'

The strategy was simple, an age-old record company ploy of, *If the original stuff isn't hooking them, stick out a cover and take it from there …* This might all sound a little calculated, but if you were up the creek for a seven-figure investment with no sign of a return any time soon, you'd probably be more than a little concerned too.

The band was as nervous about the single's success as anyone at the record company – they knew that with a fourth song missing the charts their career and record deal were certainly in jeopardy. They all met at their manager's house to await the news and erupted in ecstasy when they were told. Gary had naturally been a little disheartened when he was told they would be putting out a cover – he was proud of his own material and convinced it was worthy of success in the charts. However, he was also a realist and was happy to go along with the plan to release a cover. After all, this might have been Take That's last chance.

The single's Top Ten placing also earned the band their début *Top of the Pops* performance, a show they would eventually appear on over thirty times. However, no slot on that famous TV institution would ever have such an impact as this début appearance, which suddenly opened the floodgates of tabloid attention (despite cynical TV crew members taking bets the band couldn't actually sing). The following week, the music press and red-tops (or tabloids) swarmed all over Take That with a passion that did not dissipate until the day they finally split up.

Take That mania was starting to grip the nation.

Unfortunately, this was all too late for Korda Marshall, who was, remarkably, out of a job and watching these events from home. 'At the time I was quite bitter and twisted because I was on a royalty for Take That and M People, which I lost when I left the company, so I personally lost about half a million in cash. They said at the time that I didn't give good corporate head and I wasn't very good with accountants and lawyers. "You've spent £1.2 million and you're at No. 47 in the charts. What are you talking about?" I'd been at RCA ten years and I didn't even get a card, I didn't get a watch, I didn't get anything. There were suddenly a million people all trying to take credit for Take That, so I was written out of the script. The boys know, Nigel Martin-Smith knows, Robbie knows. Nick Raymonde signed them, I was his boss and I approved the deal, so we are both partly responsible.'

Frustrated by his treatment at RCA, Korda set up his own record label – Infectious – and proceeded to discover some heavy-hitting major acts. 'The reason I started my own company was because I couldn't get a job for over a year. The irony of ironies is that I was deemed a failure at the time because Take That were stiffing badly. If it wasn't for that I wouldn't have started my own company with some of the cash I had from being constructively dismissed by RCA, and I wouldn't have signed Muse, Ash, Garbage and everyone else.' Morphing through another label into Mushroom, Korda sold his interests as a founder in 1999 for a figure said to be several million pounds. So he doesn't exactly sit at home crying over a promo copy of 'A Million Love Songs'. He then became Managing Director of Warner Brothers Records UK and remains one of Britain's most powerful music-business executives. Everything changes.

THE MAGIC
NUMBERS

IN MAY 1992 THE BAND performed at the Children's Royal Variety Performance and even met Princess Margaret, who declared herself a fan.

Then there was time for one further single to cement Take That's growing profile before the band released their début album. 'I Found Heaven' was a chirpy pop song which notably featured the smooth-voiced Robbie Williams on lead vocals. One of the few tracks from the forthcoming album not written by Gary, the song was penned by producers Ian Levine and Billy Griffin – a heavy-on-Motown, piano-riff pop song. The video cleverly looked like it was shot in the sunny Bahamas, but was actually filmed in a wet and windy Isle of Wight. The dancing for this footage and the corresponding live routine was suitably inspired by The Drifters' and The Four Tops' own routines. However, despite the publicity they had enjoyed since their first Top Ten in June, it was a little perplexing and obviously disappointing when the song only peaked at No. 15.

Once again, Nick and the team at RCA had a battle on their hands – after all, the début album was about to come out, so slipping back in chart positions was rather untimely, as Nick Raymond explains: 'Everyone freaked out because they'd gone backwards again. However, because the band had endeared themselves to everybody – there were so many fans in the record company but also at Woolworths, WH Smiths – everyone loved these boys and this band. They went to so much trouble, the boys even travelled down to the pressing plant to meet the girls who were putting the vinyl into the sleeves at the factory. They were such hard workers, but winning people round wasn't fake, they were just genuine guys.'

According to Ian Levine, there had been an alternative choice of single recorded at the same time as 'I Found Heaven'. He recalls: 'The best song of the lot after "Could It

Be Magic?" was called "Falling for Your Girl", which I produced and wrote with Billy Griffin. It was all ready to go but then there were the arguments and it's never come out; to this day, it's never been released. I've got a copy of it with Robbie singing lead.'

However, any remaining doubts that Take That had finally broken through were shattered when they finally released their début album, *Take That and Party*, in September 1992. Although there are aspects of the album that are pure, sugary, bubblegum pop, the record certainly did not harm Gary Barlow's growing reputation as a songsmith of some ability. *Take That and Party* was a fantastic door-opener for the band. The sleeve, with the Fab Five managing the unfeasible feat of leaping, smiling and looking photogenic all at the same time, was reminiscent of The Beatles' leaping antics in their movie *A Hard Day's Night*. Musically the album was a diverse collection – cool, sensitive, rap, slow songs, fast songs, dance tunes and crooning ballads – far more sophisticated than many later boy bands that came in Take That's wake. *Take That and Party* contained a bagful of bona fide hits, and to some degree shook back to life the rotting corpse of post-Eighties pop with considerable force. While many observers in the 'serious' press belittled the band as lightweight fizz for the under-10s, the album actually still stands up today as a great dance collection mixed with some weighty ballads that more experienced writers would have been proud to release.

'ANY REMAINING DOUBTS THAT TAKE THAT HAD FINALLY BROKEN THROUGH WERE SHATTERED WHEN THEY FINALLY RELEASED THEIR DÉBUT ALBUM, *TAKE THAT AND PARTY*.'

The opening track, 'I Found Heaven', truly reflected Griffin's former role as lead singer with The Miracles, having successfully replaced the seemingly irreplaceable Smokey Robinson as lead vocalist with the silky voice of Robbie Williams. The track oozes charm, gospel handclaps and wall-to-wall soul backing vocals, giving the album a real feel-good opening. The next track up, the former single 'Once You've Tasted Love', was Gary's first writing credit on the album and his first lead vocal there too, a soul-influenced, high-energy disco track filled with advice for the Take That faithful on the subject of new love. Robbie's rap, in a deep, cod-American accent, presaged some of the self-mocking wit of his later solo work, but it fades quickly as the track comes to an early close, without quite making the impression one might have hoped.

The a cappella opening of the Top Ten smash 'It Only Takes a Minute' soon set the album back on track. It was written by Dennis Lambert and Brian Potter, who – like Billy Griffin – had had major soul success themselves, this time with The Four Tops. These retro reference points gave Take That's début album an evolved and sophisticated feel, steering the sound clear of the lightweight, linear feel of so many pop-band débuts. It was clear that this blend of Seventies and Eighties soul with Nineties disco beats was where Take That and their fan base were probably going to find their best times. Almost without breath, 'A Million Love Songs' follows, another huge hit in October 1992. Gary's yearning vocal set the pulses racing in a million young girls' hearts at the time – and it was captured in one take, perhaps reflecting the years he'd had singing the song already. It remains a classic pop song of its era, made all the more impressive by its teenage creation.

The album's fifth track, 'Satisfied', was another dance track, heavy on keyboard riff and with a solid bass line that kept the upbeat feel of the package strongly on course. Another Gary song and another Gary vocal, ably assisted by Robbie's rapping, his vocal again faintly Brooklyn-esque in tone. Robbie's contribution wound the track up, as he fades into the distance before the articulate chords of 'I Can Make It' usher in. There was already a clear distinction on the album between Robbie's fun, slightly anarchic and cool contributions, and Gary's more worthy, studied approach. In the years to come, that distinction would become more and more evident in the future solo careers of Take That's prime movers.

A slower piano ballad, 'I Can Make It', found Gary's writing balanced somewhere between Elton John and Barry Manilow, but the vocal is less histrionic than either – more Cliff Richard than Captain Fantastic – with weight added by a choir of soulful backing singers. The song presents the band not just as a bunch of party boys, but as young men capable of sensitive, understanding relationships – just what their growing audience wanted to hear.

The next track was the naïve-sounding single 'Do What You Like'. The song's up-tempo beats mask a bitter lyric, and this sense of papering over cracks in a relationship was repeated on the album's eighth track, 'Promises'. If the band drew the TV audience in with dance routines and smiles for the cameras, Gary's lyrical content was often deceptively substantial, particularly for a boy band.

'Why Can't I Wake Up with You?' was another such song. A sinuous bass line ran throughout the track, subtle rhythms building a little frame for a vocal and lyric that spoke to every teenage girl in the land on its release as a single in February 1993. The next song, 'Never Wanna Let You Go', featured a piano riff which introduced a slower, funkier, bass-driven track, darker and sensitive. The track fades slowly away, leaving a contemplative silence that is broken by the heavier groove of 'Give Good Feeling', another brisk and breezy dance mix. The feeling of fun and energy, the optimism and buoyancy of the track, sets up perfectly one of the undeniable highlights of the album, 'Could It Be Magic?'.

The final track, 'Take That and Party', was almost as though, having met the fans face-to-face with the songs so far, the boys handed them their business card, kissed them on the cheek and told them to keep in touch. It's probably the weakest track on the album – which would have felt much stronger had it ended with 'Could It Be Magic?' – but it served to remind listeners of who Take That were and of what they did.

Take That and Party was a mixture of sensitive ballads, fresh dance anthems and Motown/Philadelphia soul, blended together over dance-orientated contemporary backing. It blended well-crafted new songs with timeless classics, and offered up Gary Barlow as a songwriter of serious note, his band brimming with energy, urgency, sensitivity and, above all else, fun. And – through the subtle inclusion of 'Could It Be Magic?' – mums around the country were aware of the band too. Clever stuff.

Pop bands are not album artists, or so the music biz cliché goes. Not so Take That. Even with an album as blatantly pop as *Take That and Party*, the band showed that they were perfectly capable of shifting long-players as well as singles. The album defied the sniping critics and charted at a healthy No. 5 in the first week of September 1992, with over half a million copies being shipped out to shops in anticipation of huge demand. The album eventually managed to rise to a peak position of No. 2 and spent seventy-three weeks on the charts, a year and a half in total (the accompanying long-form video was the year's biggest seller). With contemporary No. 1 albums by the likes of Mike Oldfield (*Tubular Bells II*) and Genesis (*We Can't Dance*), as well as a rash of greatest hits albums (such as Kylie's *Greatest Hits*), the album lists were notably void of any serious new pop performers. The charts were there for the taking. On the album's release, Nigel and the boys had said that a silver disc for 60,000 sales would be a success and a gold disc for 100,000 sales would be fantastic – their ambitions were still tempered by the reality of only one of their five singles to date hitting the Top Ten. Within twelve months of going on sale, *Take That and Party* had surpassed 750,000 sales and at the time of writing is standing at 1,330,050, in excess of the quadruple-platinum mark.

Take That's momentum was kept at a breathless pace when the band hit the road for their first full headlining UK tour. It is interesting to note that the tour promoter's office was kept busy in the weeks before the shows, fielding worried calls from the band themselves, asking if he was sure they would be able to sell any tickets. It was a sell-out. Also, when the boys did a series of in-store record-shop signings to promote the album, so many people turned up to Manchester's HMV that the session had to be abandoned for safety fears as fans were starting to get crushed (later, four more HMV store appearances had to be cancelled amid similar fears). Nigel was said to be furious, saying the band hated letting their fans down and why hadn't more security been arranged by the stores?

Korda Marshall's initial gut instinct about 'A Million Love Songs' proved to be prophetically accurate in October 1992, when it became the band's second Top Ten single, also placing at No. 7 (while Korda was still out of a job). Given that Gary had written the song when he was just 15, this was no mean feat. (Gary later said he would play any new songs to his mum and nan, and if they liked them then the band would release them.)

For Nick Raymonde, who had been battling against numerous setbacks from the day he'd first signed the band, this was a genuine turning point: 'That's when it exploded, because it is a great song – and Ian Levine's version was a pretty faithful reproduction of the demo, although giving it a three-four as opposed to its original four-four time signature was a masterstroke. It actually launched the album proper, and suddenly the long-player started selling massively.'

One of Nigel Martin-Smith's shrewdest strategies as Take That's manager was his awareness of the pop market. While being one of the most lucrative, it is also the most

fickle and unforgiving. As such he made absolutely certain the growing Take That fan base did not lose focus on his protégés by maintaining a rapid-fire schedule of singles, tours, albums, TV appearances and so on. In other words, barely a week could go by when the band were not releasing products, appearing on our TVs or playing in our towns. It might sound calculated, but this was now big business. When you have a songwriter as gifted as Gary Barlow, you are able to put songs out with such regularity without compromising on the quality. It was a rare and formidable combination, and by the close of 1992 Take That was comfortably the biggest pop band in Britain.

Mark Owen has said that the moment he knew Take That had 'made it' was when they scooped a record-breaking seven trophies at the December 1992 *Smash Hits* Poll Winners' Party.

The teen magazine market was later flooded with publications, but in the early Nineties *Smash Hits* really was the biggest magazine in terms of profile and circulation, and a cover or an award was absolute confirmation that a pop band had truly made a mark on the nation's (predominantly female) teens. It was a stark barometer

of the pop nation's listening habits – notably, New Kids on the Block won nothing at that ceremony after three years of domination. According to Mark, behind the scenes was even more remarkable, with all manner of big-name artists keen to meet his band. For his part, such teen-mag awards were always a sign of Mark's own status as Take That's most popular member. There is a long list of pop bands' younger members proving to be the most popular – undoubtedly partly due to the fact that this makes them closer in age to the demographic who follow them. Boy bands straddle a difficult balance between enjoying their profile yet always appearing accessible, hence many managers insist the stars do not have girlfriends, thus making them available in some distant, theoretical fashion. *If only he catches my eye. If we wait here for another four hours for the tour bus …* Mark Owen was the epitome of that phenomenon and his house is crammed full of 'Most Fanciable Male' trophies to prove it.

The controversial and much-debated single 'Could It Be Magic?' was finally released in early December 1992, by which time Take That were easily the biggest band in Britain. The song gave them their biggest hit to date at No. 3 and sold over a quarter of a million copies in a matter of a few weeks (earning them their first silver disc in the process). The accompanying video showed the boys in an aircraft hangar made to look like some kind of pseudo-American car garage – perhaps having popped in to repair Nigel's worn-out XR3i – all dancing and singing and smiling. (The girl who switches on the light at the start and end of the video was actually a fan who won the role after writing in to *Jim'll Fix It*.)

It is rare for a pop album to enjoy longevity in the charts, but *Take That and Party* did just that when this single re-injected sales of the long-player sufficiently for it to surge past its début position of No. 5 and head all the way up to No. 2. Most impressively, the Manilow cover earned them a nomination and then an actual Brit Award in February 1993 for 'Best British Single' (perhaps an odd choice given the fact it was a cover).

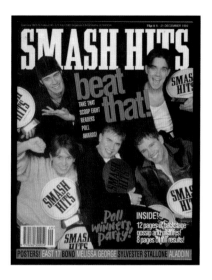

Ian Levine was no longer working with Take That but was still enjoying scores of chart hits. He'd produced hit singles for the male vocal group KWS and in December was at the *Top of the Pops* studios for their appearance to mark the Top Thirty hit 'Hold Back the Night'. Coincidentally, Take That were there to perform 'Could It Be Magic?', which Ian had been so heavily involved in at the start of the year.

'Of course I went to the boys' dressing room,' Ian told me, 'but they'd changed – back in February I said they would never change, but in my opinion they'd changed completely and they just weren't the same people any more. I just felt like I didn't know them, I felt a bit alienated.' Many years later, when Howard was a celebrity DJ, he bumped into Ian, who was invited back to Heaven nightclub to DJ at their twenty-first anniversary. 'Howard came out the DJ box and hung out with me for a while, and he was the only one of the five I ever got the chance to say "What happened?" He just shrugged his shoulders and said, "I don't know what happened. We just went along with what everyone else was doing."'

By now, Take That mania was in full flow and the band showed no intention of letting the momentum slip; in the same month as their Brit Awards triumph, they released yet another single off the album – making a total of seven from that record. 'Why Can't I Wake Up with You?' earned them their sixth chart hit and highest position to date, No. 2 (only 2 Unlimited's 'No Limit' kept them off the top spot). The last two singles alone had shifted a combined total of nearly half a million copies. The final recorded version of 'Why Can't I Wake Up with You' – one of three written when Gary was just 16 – was the result of a late-night session in those South London studios, the final cut being made at 4 a.m.

Interestingly, the band planned to penetrate America almost simultaneously with the UK, but their first forays were largely unsuccessful. The début album and the single 'It Only Takes a Minute' were released with some fanfare, but their chart positions in both cases were lowly. There was even a Take That breakfast cereal, so there was certainly no shortage of effort and money being invested, but the US is the hardest nut to crack. As Robbie would find out to his cost later in his solo years, the quirky English humour and pop sensibility that people loved so much in Blighty fell on largely deaf and disinterested ears in America.

Back at home, the band was rarely out of the papers. They were the stuff of tabloid dreams. Suddenly, however, they were not alone in the previously sparsely populated pop market. Perhaps, during the first phase of their success, Take That's biggest rivals were East 17, the quartet of rapping/singing East End boys led by former Bros manager, Tom Watkins. East 17 had hit the Top Ten with their début single 'House of Love' in August 1992, only eight weeks after Take That finally pierced the Top Ten with 'It Only Takes a Minute Girl'. Brian Harvey, singer with East 17, told me in an interview for this book how he first came across Take That: 'It was through my ex-manager, Tom. One day we were in his office and Tom was saying, "There's a group out there, a rival." But I knew nothing about them at that point. I kind of got the feeling that we weren't supposed to like this other new group.'

Releasing records at the same time and targeting the same market meant the two bands' paths would inevitably cross: 'My first recollection of ever seeing them in person was a radio roadshow down in Somerset and we were in the lobby of this hotel downstairs. It was quite busy, there were quite a lot of groups about. I was sitting in the foyer and this group of lads walked in and someone from our side of the fence said, "Oh, that's Take That." It was Howard, Jason and Mark. All I'd seen before that was the video they are probably least proud of, the one where they were having jelly pushed up their arses – obviously we all laughed at that. I was only 17 and kind of new to the industry but I'd thought, *What's that all about?* That song and that video were so far from anything I'd be doing, so, yes, we looked at them in a certain way as a result. Back in them days I wasn't really the most clued-up person – I thought I was, but I wasn't really.'

Fairly swiftly, the tabloids were full of comments about an apparent rivalry between the two bands. It was almost hyped into a variant of the class struggle, with the polished (supposedly but not actually) middle-class Take That boys coming up against the working-class East 17 bits-of-rough. Stereotypes abounded. Record sales surged. Yet Brian says there was never any real animosity between the actual band members. 'I remember being at one of the MTV after-show parties and talking to Gary very briefly. There was all this speculation about a major rivalry in the papers, but none of it was real – we didn't know them, they didn't really know us, so how could there be any tension? It suited the papers because everyone knew about Take That, so it was going to sell newspapers.'

In actual fact, despite their underdog status, East 17 would go on to enjoy a greater quantity of hits than Gary Barlow's fivesome did during the first phase of their career – Take That had fourteen Top Forty hits before they first disbanded, while East 17 had eighteen. In fact, East 17 enjoyed 228 weeks on the album and singles chart combined, compared to Take That's 118 weeks. The crucial difference was that the East London boys only enjoyed a solitary No. 1 hit, the brilliant Christmas favourite 'Stay Another Day', whereas Take That had a mighty eight chart-toppers.

'I suppose at the time I just kind of went along with it,' reflects Brian. 'It was kind of hard to make any judgement about Take That anyway because you're just in the thick of being in a boy band, you're famous and your feet ain't really on the ground. Myself, I just kind of went along with what was being said and had a bit of a laugh with it. But the fact is, I've never disliked anyone in Take That, never.'

I CAN'T BELIEVE WHAT I'M SEEING

WITH BREATHLESS RAPIDITY, THE FIRST single from Take That's second album was released just twenty weeks after the final single from their début long-player. Nonetheless, although the swiftness of the follow-up might imply a cash-in record and that more of the same was on its way, the single 'Pray' suggested otherwise.

The genesis of the single was very interesting, as Nick Raymonde explains: 'I went to Deconstruction Records [part of the RCA group] and said did they know anyone who could make a record like a Teddy Riley record. They recommended Steve Jervier, who'd done a remix for Boyz II Men. So I called up Steve and played him "Pray", which sounded a little like Simple Minds. I gave him the vocal, he came back with this amazing beat.

'I then had to sell that idea to the band, so we got all the boys into the boardroom with Nigel. I took the beat and then we chucked Gary's vocals from "Pray" over the top of it and time-stretched it ... and you could see Gary thinking *What?* at first. Then Robbie, then Howard and Mark, then Jason started to nod their heads and said they could see how sexy the dancing and video could be. Gary took his time, you could see him working things out properly, and then he said, "Yes, let's go for it!"'

In fairly stark contrast to the poppier moments on their début long-player, this new Barlow composition was slower, contemplative and yearning, while Gary's lead vocal reiterated that he was the band's kingpin. Visually, there had been a marked change too – suddenly the band looked a lot more polished and a little older (but not too old). Take That, it seemed, were about to get mature.

Whatever the aim, it worked. 'Pray' gave Take That their very first chart-topper when it hit No. 1 in July 1993. Although more recently it has become commonplace, at the time only twenty-two acts in chart history had entered at No. 1. The band were on their way to rehearse in Wales when they heard the news and Mark and Howard spent the journey getting drunk in celebration in the back of their car. The night that BBC Radio 1 announced they were No. 1 on the chart countdown, Mark taped the DJ's voice and kept rewinding it again and again to hear him say it once more.

The smooth, understated quality of the song did not go unnoticed by the music industry, who were normally prone to largely ignoring the writing efforts of boy bands. At the 1994 Ivor Novello Song Writing Awards, Gary would win the gong for 'Best Contemporary Song' and the prestigious 'Song-writer of the Year' trophy, grouping him with former winners such as Elton John, George Michael, Annie Lennox and Eric Clapton.

The video for 'Pray' was just one of many that Take That made suffering from what some call wet-boy-band syndrome. Take one good-looking boy band, put them in the shower (which they don't need because they are squeaky clean) or under a waterfall with virtually no clothes on, and hey presto, the TV channels are besieged with girls asking for repeat showings. Take That bared their fair share of flesh in their videos, and not just for 'Pray' – copious water hoses were also needed for their promo for 'Why Can't I Wake Up with You?' and their later smash single 'Back for Good'. In later years,

hilarious spoofs of the dancing-in-the-rain sequences would be perpetrated by both Ant & Dec and US punk-pop trio Blink 182, both involving watering cans and tongues planted firmly in cheeks.

'AT FIRST YOU THOUGHT,
HE NEEDS TO PAY ATTENTION.'

Around this time, former GMTV director Michael Metcalf had several behind-the-scenes experiences with the band and his eye-witness reports about the insanity of their life at this point give a fascinating insight into Planet Take That. 'I first worked with them on a Saturday morning show called *GIMME 5*. They were already fairly well established and obviously everyone was excited that we had Take That coming on the show. What was very obvious and interesting was that Robbie had already started to kind of distance himself from the rest of the band. They were all being very sensible and yet he had roller boots on, and he was whizzing round all morning. At first you thought, *He needs to pay attention*, but actually I realized he was taking everything in, plus he always made sure he was in the shot and that all eyes were drawn to him. They sang a couple of numbers on the show and of course the audience just went wild. It was amazing to see the reaction.

'When we finished the show at noon, the security and police were very concerned because they couldn't clear a road in Newcastle city centre to get them out. With their security taking charge, they went up and stood on the roof on the top floor of the car park to wave to the massive crowds below to try to ease some of the pressure and divert attention away from the roads so that an escape route could be organized. When the boys appeared on the roof, the fans went absolutely berserk.

'Nigel Martin-Smith ran things with clinical precision. It was very impressive to see. For example, the only way they'd agreed to go on the roof was on the condition that some other person was always standing between each member, so that no one could get an unauthorized shot of them all together as a band. So basically we stood them on the roof and had the floor manager standing between a couple of them, a researcher standing between the next two, and I just remember thinking at the time, *That is so sharp*.

'I met them individually and they were just really nice guys. At the time Jenny Powell was the presenter and she and Jason knew each other and were very close. They were good mates and would go out because one of Jason's brothers was Jenny Powell's accountant. I also remember one of our researchers was really taken with Jason and the following week his twin brother came up to the show and this researcher thought all her birthdays had come at once! Gary was very mild, quieter and more sensible, Mark and Howard were quiet too, whereas Robbie was just wild. I think I saw Jason at his bubbliest because he was familiar with Jenny.

'The next time I worked with them was when I had started work at GMTV a few months later. They were due to do *Top of the Pops* and we got an interview arranged with them in the dressing room. What struck me that night was how, in that very short period of time, Robbie was so much further removed from the rest of the band. He didn't seem as though he wanted to be involved in it, it was kind of surreal.'

'THEY SOLD OUT WEMBLEY ARENA IN MINUTES.'

By now, only the arena circuit could satiate demand for tickets to see Take That. The end of July 1993 saw the band's first full headlining arena tour and it was a total sell-out weeks in advance. Nick Raymonde at RCA was not alone in being amazed: 'They were unbelievable live, they were astonishing, but when someone suggested they do an arena date, it was like, "Don't be stupid, there's no way they can do an arena." Then wallop … they sold out Wembley Arena in minutes and no one expected that. You have to remember it wasn't long since they'd just been doing these club PAs, so they went from doing these big clubs to doing arenas, there wasn't any middle ground, it was a huge leap.'

What most people don't realize is just how intimately involved the five lads and Nigel were in the live shows, both financially and creatively, as Nick explains: 'They had a really good team around them so there was no expense spared. They were making so much money from the shows but they just kept pouring every spare penny back into the live sets. I've never seen anything like it. They invested so much of their own money and, of course, from a record company's point of view it was heaven.

'A lot of the ideas would come from the band. They used to sit around saying, "What can we do next on tour that is absolutely mad and spectacular?" It was all their ideas with Nigel, nothing to do with the record label. Tours sell records, so I'd go to the rehearsal and think, *Oh my God, I can't believe what I am seeing!*'

Jason and Howard's role in all this was absolutely key: 'Basically, Jason and Howard would come up with the routines with Mark, then they would show Robbie and Gary – Robbie picked them up in about five seconds, Gary always struggled a bit but in the end it didn't matter. They didn't have a choreographer who told them what to do from the start; they had people who would help them stage the show, but not what I would call a choreographer.'

This arena tour coincided with the onslaught of Take That merchandise, which went way past the usual band T-shirts to include such varied items as clocks, dolls, books, stickers, calendars, scarves, stationery and even a Take That cake – all emblazoned with the two Ts of the Take That logo. Again, this was one more example of Nigel's comprehensive management of the project, a strategy that has become something of a blueprint for future boy and girl pop bands.

Take That were the biggest band in Britain and, unbeknown to them at the time, in the middle of a run of four consecutive No. 1 hits. The chart-topping success of 'Pray' was matched in October by the boys' first collaboration, the smash hit 'Relight My Fire', which featured Scottish chanteuse Lulu on joint lead. It was a remarkable choice of partnership between the sexiest young boy band on the planet and one of pop's elder stateswomen. But Lulu's career – however much it benefited from her association with Take That – was by no means in desperate need of a boost. If anything, the benefit was to the boys themselves.

Lulu had been born Marie McDonald McLaughlin Lawrie on 3 November 1948, the daughter of a Scottish butcher. A natural showbiz gal who seemed to have been born to sing, Lulu's career had kicked off as a teen sensation in the early Sixties. After a childhood singing wherever and whenever she could, Lulu was discovered in a Glasgow disco at the age of 14 as the lead singer with proto-pop group The Gleneagles. This morphed into Lulu and the Luvvers and their release of an old Isley Brothers' hit 'Shout' as their first single was a smash hit. As with so many British bands of the time – most notably, of course, The Beatles – it was the reinterpretation of American soul classics and sounds that endeared Lulu to the home crowd – something that Take That and their producers were also often focused on.

Lulu became a major pop star with a string of hit singles. Recognized by many as one of the best white soul voices of the age, she was also the first British female singer to tour behind the Iron Curtain and even topped the US singles chart for five weeks – the first non-US woman to do so. By the mid-Eighties she was also appearing on TV regularly as an actress, notably as the mother of Adrian Mole in the hit series of the bestselling book.

With a career so broad in scope, and nearly thirty years of treading the boards behind her, Lulu's 1993 comeback single 'Independence' just missed the Top Ten. Remarkably, though, with so much success behind her already, 'Relight My Fire' was actually her first UK No. 1 single, surely one of the longest journeys for any major recording artist to have made.

The recording of the song with Lulu was problematic. Nick Raymonde laughs fondly when he recalls the circumstances: 'I wanted them to make a classic disco record and the only person I knew to do that was Joey Negro. I'd always dreamed of making a record with him, because he was like a hero in my dance days. Nigel thought it was a great idea as well. "Relight My Fire" was done in Joey Negro's own studio, and it was a nightmare. It was a shitty little studio, there was no window between the control room and where Gary was, no talk-back in the vocal booth either, so every time Joey wanted to make a point to the vocalist he had to get up and walk into the booth, tell them what to do and then walk back and start again. Yet somehow he made this extraordinary record.'

Initially, the record company were said to have wanted a black diva to sing the vocal. Nick continues, 'I was thinking we needed to get Kym Mazelle or Jocelyn Brown but Nigel suggested Lulu. I thought, *That's mad, I can't get my head round that!* But I really fancied going with it and he was so right. Really, with Nigel, he was the No. 1 pop manager: he was brilliant and uncompromising, yet at the same time he was totally open to the A&R being done how I was doing it – if he hadn't have been so perceptive and savvy, we wouldn't have made those records.'

'"RELIGHT MY FIRE" WAS ACTUALLY HER FIRST UK NO. 1 SINGLE.'

Lulu was put forward and everyone loved what they heard. The plan had been for Robbie to sing lead vocals, with Howard featuring on backing, but the combination wasn't clicking and eventually the decision was taken to go with Gary and Lulu. The song itself was a late-Seventies hit for US disco supremo Dan Hartman, whose 1978 smash 'Instant Replay' was also an instant dance-floor classic. 'Relight My Fire' had been a hit in 1979 for Hartman, with Loletta Holloway taking the female vocal; Take That's masterstroke was to have that role voiced by Lulu. It's hard to justify many songs as an instant classic, but if ever a Take That single truly deserved the accolade this was it – fun, exciting, urgent, camp: the record had it all. 'I thought it was amazing,' says Nick Raymonde. 'I couldn't believe we'd actually made this record, a classic disco record that could have existed in the Seventies but in the Nineties sounded cool on Radio 1 and in the clubs.'

The video was a sartorial car crash, with Robbie in a comedy oversized hat, like the ones you see worn by students on rag week. Mark was squeezed into a tiny cropped T-shirt emblazoned with the legend 'Junkie's Baddy Powder' and Gary donned a frightening spangled gold waistcoat with bare arms, so the various cavorting transvestites and weird characters seemed tame by comparison. Still, the clip found itself on heavy rotation on all the terrestrial TV channels so no one seemed to care. Thirty years into

her career, Lulu was by far the sexiest of the six singers on stage when the band appeared on *Top of the Pops* with her. Sadly, a year or so after the song's rebirth writer Hartman died, aged 46.

One other combination that has passed into Take That folklore is that of Jason and Lulu, who for years were rumoured to have lit each other's fires. Suitably respectful coyness followed, and both parties denied they had ever slept together.

Just two weeks after the single and just over a year since the début album, Take That maintained their prolific output with their second album, entitled *Everything Changes*. And everything did change with this release, not least in terms of image. Gone were the whacky, leaping, bare-chest-and-leather boys of *Take That and Party*, and in came five boys in pure white on the intimate sleeve. Most of the tracks were written by Gary this time around. The album opener was, naturally, 'Everything Changes'. As on *Take That and Party*, it was a Robbie vocal that opened the album, a low, sexy voice somewhere between Staffordshire and Los Angeles. 'Everything Changes' was mature pop from Barlow and co-writers Mike Ward, Eliot Kennedy and Cary Baylis, and the track remains a huge favourite with all the fans who danced away Christmas 1993 to its sophisticated arrangement, driving bass lines and hooky backing vocals. That said, compared to his latter-day performances, Robbie's voice still sounds somewhat immature (and in the video he looks about 10). Many thought that the second song, 'Pray', was the best track on the album, a slow-burner that was perfect for increasing Take That's audience beyond girls (and some boys) and into the ranks of mums (and some dads).

Gary sang lead vocal again on 'Wasting My Time', heavy on Philadelphia soul with funky guitar breaks and horn stabs throughout another fantastic arrangement that the Jacksons would have been proud of. Gary was singing with real confidence by this point, and the boys sounded truly accomplished. Track four was the smart soul remake, 'Relight My Fire', followed by 'Love Ain't Here Anymore' – a silky smooth ballad after the urgency of 'Relight My Fire', a song about regret and remorse sung by a sensitive Gary Barlow (it's said to be Elton John's favourite Take That track). This kind of writing was demonstrating Gary's increasing ability to craft songs, and the band's ability to record a variety of styles in a variety of moods, to sequence an album intelligently and to understand the needs of the listening audience. Their subtle leaps from hyper dance track to perceptive love song meant that Take That were always going to be more than simply a one-trick boy band. This skill was clearly marked as the soul mood was kept slow and easy on track six, 'If This is Love', which was notable as Howard's first co-writing credit (with producer David James). Reflecting Howard's love of dance music and DJ-ing, the song is one of the funkiest grooves on the album, but Take That's echoes of US soul are still evident throughout the song. For Howard fans old and new, it is a favourite.

'TAKE THAT WERE ALWAYS GOING TO BE MORE THAN SIMPLY A ONE-TRICK BOY BAND.'

Gary was back at the helm for 'Whatever You Do to Me', another horns and keyboard-driven, mid-tempo soul track. 'Meaning of Love' was a return to the dance floor, while 'Why Can't I Wake Up with You?' contained a bagful of interesting studio sounds that moved the essentially thoughtful and contemplative song along really smoothly. 'You Are the One' set a million bedroom floorboards jumping again, with ace disco beats and smart vocals from Gary, another great example of Take That's sense of melody and ease with vocal harmony and groove. 'Another Crack in My Heart', a track written by Gary in his mid-teens, perfectly fitted in with Gary's more recent role as singer-songwriter on the piano, reminiscent of some of Cliff Richard's late Eighties/early Nineties hits.

As the album came towards the end, 'Broken Your Heart' was the jaunty penultimate song. Back to the disco, back to the string accompaniments and backing vocals of

'Relight My Fire', it set the closing track up perfectly. Amid telephone-call sound effects and a moody, dark opening, 'Babe' was a *tour de force* with which to close the album. It was the longest track on the album, a gorgeous arrangement, a heartbreaking lyric and a crystal-clear lead vocal from Mark to close the record down. The increasingly emotional closing bars of the song left the Take That listener drained at the end of their superb second album, another amazing and eclectic collection of pop songs, ballads and dance tracks that proved their number-one status at the time.

The band's A&R man, Nick Raymonde, gave me a fascinating insight into how the songwriting process was working at this point: 'I'd sort of got into a routine with Gary where he would give me the demos of his songs that he'd recorded at home and then I would strip out the vocal and send it out to my network of producers, songwriters and remixers for ideas about treating it differently. What was very impressive was the fact that both Gary and Nigel were really cool about this. That is rare. Great songwriters are often very precious, but Gary was open to ideas. They were totally up for it, and that made my job really easy.'

If ever there was a pop formality, then Take That's second album was it. Sure enough, *Everything Changes* débuted at No. 1 in late October 1993. Eventually the record would boast six Top Five singles, three of which were No. 1s. Sales were staggering, selling in excess of 300,000 – platinum status – within five working days. At the time of writing, over 1.2 million copies have been bought, achieving quadruple platinum status.

THE GOLDEN YEARS

BY NOW, TAKE THAT WAS a genuine phenomenon. For a period between July 1993 ('Pray') and August 1995 ('Never Forget'), they ruled the charts. During this phase, which was the commercial and also creative zenith of the first incarnation of the band, the boys enjoyed seven consecutive No. 1 singles, another No. 3 single and two No. 1 albums, shifting millions of copies of both formats all round the globe.

'THEY WERE NOW THE BIGGEST BAND IN THE UK.'

'Babe' was the first single to follow the album's release, but fans already owning the song had no impact whatsoever on its massive sales, with over 600,000 copies selling, making it Take That's second-biggest-selling single of their career at that point – as well as a song that ramped up their profile even more in Europe. Despite the very sophisticated festive video showing Mark and the boys in a Russian-like landscape, the excellent song actually lost out on the coveted Christmas No. 1 spot to Mr Blobby. Matters were back on course when the album's title track hit No. 1, although the follow-up, 'Love Ain't Here Anymore', stalled just short at No. 3, hardly a failure. Besides, the No. 1 song that week – and for four months – was Wet Wet Wet's record-breaking single 'Love is All Around'.

In the middle of these three singles the band performed for one of their highest-profile TV slots ever, the 1994 Brit Awards. It was particularly pleasing that they were now the biggest band in the UK and were fêted to perform, whereas they had previously been snubbed altogether. Their choice of songs raised a few eyebrows – a Beatles medley complete with the boys wearing suitably Sixties costumes – but they insisted that

they were merely paying tribute to the Fab Four, rather than comparing themselves to McCartney & Co.

Of course, no one would suggest that Take That are culturally as important as The Beatles, and their record sales are obviously dwarfed by those of the Fab Four, as are their chart histories. However, there is a genuine comparison to be had in the hysteria of the fans and the mass popularity the That-ers enjoyed during their absolute peak. Jewellery was ripped off, ears/arms/private parts pulled, eyes poked, hair grabbed … mob behaviour with good intentions. There was even a tank on one Far Eastern runway to escort them to safety.

With total domination of the UK pop market complete, Take That inevitably wanted to expand their horizons, and in the spring of 1994 they set out on their first headline tour of Europe. Gary came back for these dates looking fitter than ever, and pinned his keenness to lose weight on being upset by the Spitting Image puppet version of himself, which was far from flattering. 'I love my food,' he once admitted. 'I love a good curry … always up for a good Ruby. I like Italian and I like cheese and onion Ringos. I could eat ice cream by the gallon and I did try to give up chocolate once, but I only lasted a few months.' He made no secret that he found being constantly surrounded by four very fit and handsome guys quite intimidating; which is a shame, really, given that he was the musical and creative nucleus around which the whole band was formed. He also scotched rumours that his newfound physique was in preparation for an imminent solo career.

'THERE WAS EVEN A TANK ON ONE FAR EASTERN RUNWAY TO ESCORT THEM TO SAFETY.'

By the time the boys hit the road, shows selling out in minutes was a matter of course. With no sign of their fame dwindling, the tabloids were still keen to cover every aspect – literally – of the band's shows both in Europe and back in the UK in August. When Howard chose to wear chaps that revealed quite a few square inches of bottom flesh, the tabloids went crazy. 'Horny!' yelled the *Daily Star*, 'Cheeky Devil!' trumpeted the *Daily Express*, the general consensus being that Howard had overstepped the mark on what was acceptable, given that the band's audience contained predominantly teenage and pre-teen girls. The red-tops reported appalled mums dragging their children from venues, covering their eyes in horror at the 'near-pornographic' content of the show.

Howard's tour problems continued in Berlin, when he performed his usual flip and landed awkwardly, breaking the middle finger on his left hand. He said he'd never been in so much pain but he eventually finished the show and had it splinted afterwards, before going outside to meet fans and sign autographs.

Another problem the band had was when Robbie took to sucking a dummy on occasion. He later claimed it was just a whim when he'd turned up for a photo-shoot with a spot on his chin, but the tabloids were soon reading far more sinister implications into the odd habit. At the time, ecstasy was the drug of choice for thousands of ravers around Britain, and many sucked dummies to help keep themselves hydrated (it makes you chew and thus create saliva). The press were quick to jump on the connection and ride it for all it was worth. Take That's teenage fans started mimicking Robbie, and dummies were selling like they'd never done before, with some manufacturers struggling to cope with demand. Given this disturbing development and mindful of how inappropriate it could look, Robbie issued a vehement denial in the papers that he used drugs and discontinued his dummy-sucking: 'I don't take drugs and I have no interest in them at all.'

Both these instances reflected the band's continued attempts to reinvent their look and reshape their image. Howard was one of the few white men who could wear dreadlocks

and get away with it; Jason's facial hair became his trademark; Robbie's hair changed colour weekly; Mark was always the pretty one whatever their image portrayed; and Gary struggled to pin down an outfit that he looked really comfortable in.

Nick Raymonde states categorically that the band did not have a stylist who dressed them in clothes they didn't like: 'They were cool guys. They chose their own clothes. Robbie always knew what hat to wear and what T-shirt to wear. Sometimes if you needed to take a quick photo-shoot, a stylist would go with them to the shops, get hundreds of clothes then chuck them into the middle of a room, but they would pick what they wanted. They had a natural sense of what to wear.'

By now Take That really was the biggest pop band in Europe, and most of the world – the Far East, Japan, South America and Australasia – also fell under their spell. At their very peak, the record company was receiving 10,000 phone calls a week about them, often requiring receptionists to go on Take That duty; their official fan club boasted over 70,000 paid-up members; the database of fans details extended to 300,000 names and is said to have been the basis for BMG's entire data-collection policy in future years. 'We pretty much had every single person who ever bought a Take That single,' explained Nick Raymonde, 'their e-mail or postal address, where they lived, what they drove, what their parents did for a living, everything about them really. It was unique.'

The year 1994 was capped off perfectly when the band scooped even more trophies at the prestigious and highly influential *Smash Hits* awards. These included gongs for 'Best Group', 'British Group', 'Single' ('Sure'), and 'Pop Video' ('Sure'), as well as 'Best Dressed Man' (Mark), 'Most Fanciable Star' (Mark) and 'Best Haircut' (Robbie). This complemented their MTV Award for 'Best Group', which was a genuine reflection of their omnipresence in the European charts.

Oddly, MTV were slow to pick up on the boys' popularity. Or rather, they were aware of their success but chose not to play their videos too often. Nick Raymonde, formerly of RCA, explained this to me more: 'Even once they'd sold three or four million records, MTV still wouldn't put their videos on. In the end what happened was Nick Godwin and Nicki Chapman, RCA's Head of Promotion and Head TV plugger

respectively, were told by MTV, "We don't think it's our audience." We just said, "Well, why don't you have Take That's audience as well?" Eventually they saw the logic, and pretty soon Take That became huge on MTV, absolutely massive: you couldn't turn it on without seeing Take That!'

'THE PRESSURES OF FAME CAN BUILD VERY QUICKLY.'

Their huge popularity meant the boys were constantly being asked to raise funds for/awareness of numerous charities. They were always delighted to help, although this only ever added to their already exhausting schedules. The band represented and helped raise funds for countless charities fighting child poverty, AIDS and so on, but perhaps their favourite fundraiser was for the Bryan Robson Scanner Appeal, which meant they got to play with the actual Manchester United team at Old Trafford (they once gave all the profits from a massive Manchester arena show to this charity). One other story concerned a young female fan in a coma – Mark was out of the country at

the time but recorded a message on a tape, and when it was played at her bedside she woke up.

Under such a microscope, the pressures of fame can build very quickly. The very first signs that there might have been chinks in the band's seemingly impenetrable armour came with a piece in the *Sun* saying that Take That had considered quitting, concerned that their time in the spotlight was drawing to a close and that they were exhausted. The problem for members of any big band is that any hint of a complaint or even mild displeasure is immediately perceived by the press and many fans as an ungrateful whinge. To be fair, to a radio listener working long hours in a hot and dangerous factory, a pop star saying they are exhausted is always going to grind; but that doesn't mean they aren't working outrageously hard.

Brian Harvey from rival boy band East 17 spoke to me about such pressures: 'My manager described it to me like this; he said, "It's like a ball rolling down a hill: once it goes, you can't stop it." I must have heard that expression a thousand times. They'd say, "It's like a ball rolling down a hill, Brian," and I used to think *Fuck off. I just want a night off, I'm knackered.'*

Shane Lynch from Irish band Boyzone gives a very interesting insight into the workload Take That would have been subjected to. 'I tell you what, not a lot of partying gets done until you go on tour and you've got time to stay up late. There are endless hours of promotional tours. I think in one year we did something crazy like 135 flights, and Take That were probably doing even more. That's a plane flight every few days for a year. Both Take That and Boyzone did three countries in one day on numerous occasions. It's ludicrous. At some points, you're so tired you're hallucinating. You don't know who you are, your own name. You cry for no reason, you're emotionally drained. You haven't a clue. The picture is painted very nicely when you're on stage at *Top of the Pops*, and you're quite tired really and people think you go home and that's all you do. Folks have no idea whatsoever.'

One common feature of boy-band work is that they often receive a wage, in Take That's case around £150 a week during the early days (press reports usually neglected to mention the large lump sums sensibly stashed away by their management gathering interest on the band's behalf). Obviously this changes once royalties come in, and, to be fair, many pop managers see this as a way of preventing a set of very young men from going off the rails.

'TAKE THAT WERE A BOY BAND ADORED BY TEENAGE GIRLS THE WORLD OVER.'

Like all members of the band, Robbie saw repercussions of his fame at home – fans would hang around outside his mum's shop, making it an intimidating and off-putting experience for customers. Graffiti declaring fans' love was written over any house even vaguely associated with the band, and when Robbie's mum came to sell her house she found she had literally dozens of viewings straight away, but nearly all of the 'buyers' turned out to be young teenage girls.

Much has been made of Nigel's boot camp regime, with tales of weight control, girlfriends being banned, midnight curfews and strict codes of conduct. Unless you were in the band you would not know the full extent of this, but this was not new in pop, nor was it out of place. Weight is, rightly or wrongly, a part of a band's image, and the media and public will judge certain genres of music as much on their visual impact as on their sound. Take That were a boy band adored by teenage girls the world over: image was always going to be crucial.

But Nigel's attention to detail went beyond just the band and their career. Conscious of the fact that thousands of young, pre-teen and teenage girls were travelling to see the band, hanging around city centre hotels and outside venues late at night, Nigel arranged – at the band's and his own cost – to have extra security put on to patrol for

perverts. There was one reported occurrence of a young girl being approached and asked to go to a hotel room by a stranger, but because of Nigel's vigilance this was thankfully an isolated incident.

By now, by Gary's own admission, if they 'put out a record with burping on it, it would probably be a hit'. That may have been true, but the pressure was on Take That to come back with a quality opening single for their next album campaign, and not just chart fodder. Once again, the boys hit the mark for two weeks with the infectious 'Sure', released in October 1994 as Take That approached the very peak of their popularity. When they met Princess Diana ahead of appearing at her Concert of Hope for World Aids Day, she admitted she was a big fan; Mark responded by asking her out on a date, which was politely declined. Later, at the Royal Variety Performance, they met the Royal Other Half.

Although the new single only sold 30,000 copies more than 'Love Ain't Here Anymore', this was enough to lift it to No. 1, the band's fifth in fifteen months. The song was co-written by Gary, Mark and Robbie, with Gary taking the lead vocal on a soulful melody that was proof of the band's increased maturity. The promo video for the track was an odd Monkees-like home video, showing the boys all living together, Mark making the dinner, others sleeping and fooling about – Robbie had gone to get the shopping – while trying to look after an angelic blonde girl aged about 6. The video also contained the band's worst look since the undeniable nadir of 'Do What You Like', when they performed a dance routine in black mesh tops – only 'The Body' of Howard Donald could carry it off, the rest of them looked uncomfortable and awkward. Strangely, given their profile and success, when 'Sure' lost its No. 1 slot after three weeks the band briefly thought about splitting up, a sign of just how high expectations around Take That had become.

More dates around Europe followed, while work began on the studio sessions for the band's third album, to be called *Nobody Else*, due for release in August 1995. No. 1 in the UK was inevitable for Take That now, but their next single was something special. Entitled 'Back for Good', the song has to go down as one of the great British pop singles. Remarkably, it is based around just four simple chords, a challenge Gary set himself to meet when he sat down to write the track. Initially Mark had been lined up to sing lead, but eventually Gary took the role and he sounded at his absolute best. The strings were recorded at Abbey Road and the rest at producer Chris Porter's home studio. Gary said it only took him fifteen minutes to write, including a coffee break.

Nick Raymonde remembers the first time he heard it: 'After a gig we'd often go back to the hotel. Frequently, there'd be a piano in a lobby and we'd all end up singing songs, like being part of a really nice family, sitting around singing Take That songs. Then after people went to bed Gary would sometimes play me a new idea. One night he said, "Nick, here's something I'm just working on. What do you think?" Then he played me "Back for Good". I couldn't believe what I was hearing.'

The song was a monster hit. It deserved every accolade it ended up winning (and there were plenty) – the acoustic guitar intro, the string arrangement, the call-and-response soul vocals, the late-night lyrics, the heart and soul of the piece: everything combined to produce a song that any writer could base a career on, that any band could immediately claim as a classic. It is undoubtedly one of – if not *the* – musical highlights of Take That's (and, by definition, Gary Barlow's) career. Gary later said this song was the pinnacle of the band's career, and it would be hard to argue with that. Their record company, RCA, were suitably impressed, cemented by a show-stopping performance at that year's Brit Awards, and offered them a new four-album £20 million deal.

Sales were so massive – eventually surpassing nearly 800,000 copies – that at one point the rest of the Top Ten records' sales added together and then doubled were still short of what the song was shifting. It was an international smash too, hitting the No. 1 spot in an incredible thirty-one countries. Of course, the classic video shot at Pinewood Studios helped sell thousands more copies and is perhaps the band's finest moment on celluloid. Dancing alongside an old American car in the rain, the boys looked stylish, sexy and super-cool. There are moments when Robbie in particular looks like the coolest pop star on earth. Elsewhere, Howard's lithe dancing in that odd furry bear hat seems to contort his body into seemingly impossible shapes.

'Back for Good' won Gary yet more Ivor Novello Awards, including 'Best Song Musically and Lyrically', the PRS 'Most Performed Work', plus two further nominations for 'Best Selling Song/International Hit of the Year'. Ever aware of the importance of his fan base, Gary thanked the panel for the awards but later added, 'These awards are voted for by only a few people in the record industry, and at the end of the day it's what the public think. They're the most important part of all of this.'

Perhaps most excitingly, 'Back for Good' had finally managed to send Take That into the top end of the US charts, where the single was a *Billboard* Top Ten hit (the main music chart in the US). How that came about is typical of the complicated behind-the-scenes environment that Take That's success engendered. Nick Raymonde, Nigel Martin-Smith and Take That's then-lawyer John Kennedy flew out to speak to prospective new record labels. 'It was very kind of them to invite me,' recounts Nick, 'to meet up with record labels who were interested in signing Take That. "Back for Good" was exploding all over the world at this point. The head of Arista was Clive Davis, in my opinion the best A&R man in the universe. Before we were due to meet other labels, we went to speak with Clive. We walked in and he said, "Listen to this amazing record," and played "Back for Good". We were like, "Yeah, Clive, we've heard this a million times …" but then he got to the end and said, "Let's listen to it again. Isn't it amazing?" This is one of the most powerful men in the world of music, so we listened again. Then he said, "I'd like you to meet a few people," and escorted us down the corridor and into the boardroom, where we were confronted by the entire staff of the record company. He played the record again and then the video and said, "Now I'm going to watch it again." I was thinking, *This guy is going to break this band on his own!* He was an amazing character.'

American radio picked up on the song, and music channels over there loved the video. The band's legacy of mimicking The Beatles appeared to be stepping up a gear – finally, after years of work, they were primed and ready to conquer the States.

It never happened. Within three months, Robbie Williams was no longer a member of Take That.

I DON'T EVEN
LIKE MELON

WHILE 'BACK FOR GOOD' WAS quite literally ruling the world's charts, Robbie Williams was escalating out of control. In late 2005 he said on the ITV1 documentary *Take That – For the Record* that as soon as he realized he couldn't be sacked, 'That was when they lost me. I can't be sacked. Let's do drugs.' The other four boys themselves admitted that their on-the-road lifestyle was not necessarily as squeaky clean as people might have imagined. In interviews with the media at the time, every single member would always say their favourite place to be was at home with family and friends, which it probably was, but they admitted in the documentary that the time spent on the road was not all about pining in the tour bus with only a photo of their family for company. Howard was quoted as saying, 'I was naughty, you know, everyone was, everyone had a good time, we all had our share.' Gary said there were queues of girls waiting for them everywhere; and Jason denied they were not allowed female friends, only no full-time girlfriends. Mark said they were five show-offs and the adulation was welcome, making them super-charged. There has also been talk of wanking competitions on the tour bus, spliffing up, and Mark chuckling about even popping the odd ecstasy tablet while partying in a Spanish club.

However, at the time, they were understandably eager not to upset fans or fans' parents – take this quote from Gary in their official 1995 annual: 'After a gig, I get to the hotel psyched-up from being on stage and get stuck into *Homes and Interiors* magazine.' (You can almost hear Sid Vicious turning in his grave.) Elsewhere, the tabloids started rubbing their hands together with glee when rumours suggested Mark Owen, the man christened 'Angel' by his fans, was receiving medical treatment for dehydration. A hundred clever headlines were scrapped, however, when it transpired this was because he'd spent too long in a sauna. That said, the *Sun* did quote Gary as saying he had a girl in every port, but the Take That PR machine managed to gloss over this fairly quickly.

Korda Marshall says that, in the early days at least, they were genuinely clean-living: 'They were clean and healthy and good-looking, they were in tune with their bodies and very fit. They would all spend a lot of the time in the gym, Gary included.' Some of the boys 'used to like to smoke weed and then giggle', Robbie admitted on the ITV1 documentary, but this was not an act that would ever challenge Mötley Crüe in the bacchanalian stakes. However, it has since transpired that Robbie was the exception to the band rule, and found himself slipping fairly rapidly into vices that would temporarily overpower him.

Robbie's lifestyle choices were starting to concern people around and within the band throughout the year before he actually left Take That. Many years later, he admitted himself that 'before Take That I'd done acid, speed and smoked a lot of weed so I was sort of heading in that direction anyway,' but this was not known at the time, so to see the youngest member of this top boy band spiral into such hedonism was a shocking sight.

Nigel Martin-Smith tells one story where the boys were playing the inaugural MTV Awards ceremony in Berlin and when he flew in he found Robbie the worse for wear after partying heavily all night with a famous supermodel. Robbie had always been Take That's joker – the rollerblading comedian with the funny faces, the red hair or number 1 shaved into his scalp, so there were regular signs that he was no dull boy. When he was offered £130,000 to pose nude for a women's magazine he said it was £65,000 per inch. Robbie carries the odd duality of being very cocky and simultaneously very self-deprecating. He once said he was shitting himself that kiss-and-tell stories would ruin his self-esteem, but then in the same sentence he delighted in the fact that 'two people sold their stories about me and they're the only two people in the world that I've ever done a good performance with!' For the record, one story gave him eleven out of ten in bed. 'I hope that my mates read it,' was all he had to say. 'Bob from Stoke, Give Us a Poke', cried the banners in Take That's audience.

Songwriters' manager Stephen Budd was always surprised by Robbie's self-assuredness in company: 'I remember being with Robbie and Stephen Fry and Keith Allen at the Groucho Club quite a lot and the amazing thing is how he was so young and yet he could hold his own with those guys. To hold your own wit with people like that is something else.'

Robbie was the laugh-machine, always fooling around, always jovial. But hearing rumours and whispers that Robbie was drinking heavily and partying even harder was very different, and compared to the light-hearted times we knew him for, it felt somehow quite sinister. Robbie said as much himself when he revealed he often downed a bottle of vodka a day at the age of only 19. 'I was so depressed,' he told the 2005 ITV1 documentary, 'going back to my hotel in Manchester, and I'd just drink myself to oblivion, wailing like a banshee in my room by myself.' Robbie also said in the documentary that he would have taken the drugs with or without Take That.

Famously, the most public example of Robbie's downward spiral was when he went to the Glastonbury Festival in the summer of 1995. He'd been to the legendary festival the year before but that time had largely stuck to strict band rules – he was escorted by security, gave no interviews unless they were pre-approved and spent a lot of his weekend in the sanctuary of M People's tour bus. One year on and how things had changed …

'I was standing backstage at Glastonbury when this Rolls-Royce turned up,' recalls Korda Marshall, 'and the door opened and Robbie fell out of it holding three bottles of champagne. I was standing right there by the car and Robbie said, "Korda! What the fuck are you doing here?" and I said, "Robbie, what the fuck are you doing?" Then he disappeared off with his mates and that was that. He was in a state, but for me he had every right to be in a state: he'd gone through the mangle of pop and ultimately rebelled against it.'

'ROBBIE WAS THE LAUGH-MACHINE, ALWAYS FOOLING AROUND, ALWAYS JOVIAL.'

Pictures in virtually every newspaper showed the bleached-blond singer draped across Liam Gallagher of Oasis, dancing on stage with Oasis, and all the time clearly worse for wear and, apparently, missing a tooth (he later revealed he'd just drawn black pen on it). When questioned about his gap-toothed grin, he said, 'Kids the length and breadth of the country will have this soon.' Worse still, in complete contravention of the strictly controlled environment surrounding the band, Robbie gave out unofficial interviews to pretty much anyone who asked him a question. Seeing an ultra-famous boy-band member obviously caning it backstage at Glastonbury and happily chatting to anyone who approached him was a trouble magnet of the most extreme kind. He recounted how he'd got a dozen bottles of champagne and slung them into the boot of his car and driven to the festival site; he said that when Liam Gallagher first saw Robbie, Liam said, 'Take fucking what?' The band's press office must have been crying into their coffees the next morning.

Robbie hung out with Oasis, drank a lot, laughed a lot and fell over a lot. He introduced himself to Pulp by reciting one of his poems (he has said he wanted to release a collection of poems tentatively entitled *Bob through the Kitchen*). Rather sadly, Robbie claims to have virtually no recollection of that weekend at all, although the hundreds of embarrassing photographs taken by the paparazzi and festival-goers serve to offer ample reminders. If there was any mystery surrounding Robbie's personal issues previous to this weekend in Somerset, by the time the papers hit the newsstands on the Monday morning the whole sordid situation was public knowledge. This was June. In August there was scheduled to be a new single and album, followed by extensive tour dates. But by 17 July, a handful of days later, Robbie was no longer a member of Take That.

Little did anyone know at the time, but those concerts would be going ahead without Robbie Williams. It seems hard to imagine, perhaps, to fans of post-millennial pop, that if Girls Aloud or McFly split up it would have such an impact on the day's news. However, at the time, Robbie leaving Take That was a genuinely massive shock. It was heralded with a full-on newsflash on many television channels. Radio programmes were interrupted and late editions of papers altered. It was *that* big.

Of course, there had been rumours for weeks. No band can have such a profile and start falling apart at the seams without some indication of problems. By this stage, Take That were a multi-million-pound corporation and that meant many hundreds of people were involved, dozens intimately. Leaks were bound to emerge. Still, it was a massive shock when the news was confirmed.

Distraught fans were quickly reassured by the remaining (and newly christened by some, without a hint of irony) Fab Four that they would be continuing and the upcoming arena tour was not in doubt. Fans were told that they could get a refund if they felt they were missing out now that Robbie had left. As it was, the entire tour remained a sell-out and virtually no one asked for their money back. The official statement said that Robbie was no longer able to give Take That the commitment they needed. It seemed to answer so few of the pressing questions.

WHAT HAD HAPPENED?

For years the reasons and exact details of his departure remained shrouded in mystery and tainted by the legal cases that followed. By late 2005, with the remaining four members having re-formed, more details emerged as to the rift that caused the biggest pop band in the world to begin to fall apart at the seams.

The apparent tension between Gary and Robbie back then is the stuff of music-biz legend now, but at the time of Robbie's departure only close insiders knew of this friction. As their A&R man, Nick Raymonde was involved in the personal politics on a day-to-day basis. 'There was always a dynamic in the group – even from when they started – that was quite an awkward politic to address. I would explain it like this: from a marketing point of view, Take That was a brilliant creation by Nigel. You had Mark, the guy who all the girls wanted to marry, he wasn't a threat, he was the sweetest bloke you've ever met in your life – to this day I'd say Mark is the nicest person in the world, *ever*! Gary Barlow was the ideal husband, a good, solid, conservative chap, probably didn't drink, probably didn't smoke and was just a generally good guy; Jason and Howard were the smouldering sexual element that would appeal more to the older demographic of girls and possibly the mothers of the youngest girls; and finally you had Robbie, lairy, all over the place, anything could happen in the next half-hour sort of personality.

'That was the band make-up, so when you look at it like that, it was always going to be Gary and Robbie who clashed. Looking back, you knew that once the boys grew up their natural personalities would stretch and there would probably be a breaking point. Don't forget, Mark and Rob were very young when they signed and those years between 16 and 20 are crucial in your development, so many things change.

'Also, because Gary was the songwriter, it was critical that he was always, in a sense, given "special treatment", because as the record-company man I had to have him giving me these songs. Without "Pray" and "Back for Good" and all those great songs he wrote, you didn't really have the unique concept that Take That represented. Yet I knew whilst I was doing that I was inherently alienating the other members of the band, but it was a decision that I was forced into making. I was always going to spend

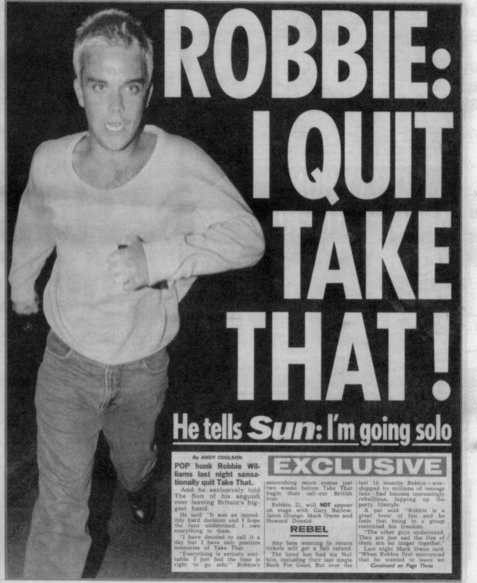

more time with Gary than with Robbie, because he was writing the songs. So I would be round at Gary's house but I wouldn't be round at Robbie's house, I wouldn't be round at Mark's, I wouldn't be round at Howard's or Jason's. I knew there would be a price to pay at some point.

'Pretty much from day one I realized what was going to happen: when it got to the point they were doing really well, I just wasn't able to give them the same amount of attention, because I was having to protect what was at the time the "crown jewels", Gary Barlow. It was always going to be Gary and Robbie that clashed and you could see that was ultimately going to end in tears.'

It wasn't just the personality clash, however: Robbie's increasingly Bohemian lifestyle and habits were said to be causing practical difficulties for a band that was run with military precision and expert professionalism. Schedules were frantic and drinking heavily or partying late was not conducive to the exhausting demands of life in the world's premier boy band.

The exact circumstances of Robbie leaving are still a little hazy, but suffice to say the remaining members now feel they should have helped Robbie a little more. Gary Barlow has said he feels they 'ganged up' on him too much. In a Territorial Army barracks-cum-rehearsal room in Cheshire, shortly after Glastonbury, the four other members said to Robbie, 'We've been thinking about doing the next tour as a four piece. What do you think?' In the ITV1 documentary in late 2005 Robbie explained his departure thus: 'I picked up a melon and said, "Can I take this?" and everyone laughed. I walked across the room and got to the door and thought, *This is it* ... and I walked through the door and then left it a few seconds and jumped back through the door and everyone laughed and ... I left ...'

Gary Barlow has admitted that he had no idea this would be the last time he would meet Robbie Williams on friendly terms for over thirteen years. At the time Gary maintained a quiet reserve surrounding the split, but when pressed he occasionally spoke openly about the problems. 'Robbie had a very different agenda. We were a very energetic young group.' Brian Harvey of East 17 could see how tensions might have arisen: 'I could sense that there was a real deep tension between Robbie and Gary. You could see it clearly: Gary takes the more considered approach, he seems together in his head; the problem is, if you're on tour with someone like that, you can begin to feel he thinks he knows it all. I can't speak for Robbie that this was how he felt but I have been in a similar position myself.'

Robbie was interviewed on TV shortly afterwards saying that although he cried when he left he had to go because he was 'tired of people's egos and their mind games'.

'And you know what?' Robbie later told *The Face*. 'I don't even like melon.'

NOBODY BETTER

THE DUST OVER ROBBIE'S DEPARTURE from Take That would take many years to settle, and involved lawyers, newspapers and the key players themselves for some time to come before any kind of resolution and reconciliation would occur. However, in the immediate aftermath of his leaving the band the remaining four members had a single, an album and a massive tour to promote. They were heavily invested in the shows' sets and production and as a band they wanted to play these dates for their fans.

The early August 1995 release, 'Never Forget', was the last Take That single to feature Robbie, and was released only a couple of weeks after he'd left. Another No. 1, another strong song and brilliant, retrospective video. Home videos of the boys as toddlers were interspersed with fan clips, touring shots and other behind-the-scenes filming. Howard took lead vocal and completely pulled it off, justifying the faith Gary had in him when he brought the song in one day and said, 'Listen, Howard, this is one for you.'

The original mix was by Brothers in Rhythm but everyone was looking for a less spacey feel. How the final version was created is one of the most bizarre and fantastical stories in Take That's entire history. Nick Raymonde was there for the whole ride: '"Never Forget" was the most extraordinary record I've made ever in my life. When me, Nigel and John Kennedy were on our way to meet Clive Davis in that cab in New York around the time of "Back for Good", I played them the demo of "Never Forget". I said, "Gary's just written this. I think this could be a huge single but I can't work out who to get to produce it." Their lawyer John Kennedy said, "You know who should do that? Jim Steinman!"'

Nick was flabbergasted at John's suggestion, and he was right to be. Steinman is one of the music industry's legendary producers, the man behind Meat Loaf's *Bat Out*

of Hell album as well as hit records by Bonnie Tyler, a man famous for his operatic production values and painstaking attention to detail. At that moment in time he was probably the producer you would least expect to see working with a famous pop band.

'I said, "He's Meat Loaf's producer, he won't even look at it." John said, "We're friends. Do you want me to get him on the phone?" So John called him up there and then in the cab.

'"Hi Jim, John here, you OK? Listen, I've got this track by a band called Take That I'd like you to listen to …"

'"Take That? I'm a massive fan! I'd love to hear it."'

Nick Raymonde's experience of making the track was even more bizarre. It took nearly a month to make and cost £130,000. 'It was unbelievable but it didn't matter because by this time the band were so huge the record company didn't care what I spent on making the record – this was Jim Steinman after all! I just thought this was the best idea ever.

'Jim is nocturnal so you'd go to the studio at eight or nine at night and the first thing you'd do was have breakfast. He had two studios running at the same time for nearly four weeks. One studio downstairs, which had the top mixing engineer in America plus four programmers, musicians and fuck knows what else in there, then Jim would be upstairs with me in this really massive studio, which apart from the desk only had one small collection of items in the middle of this huge studio floor – four sets of absolutely tiny little speakers and a chair.

'I'd walk into the studio and there'd be a bit of a bass line and some children singing and that would be all there would be; he would send that to the mixing people downstairs, then they would mix that whole section and send it back up to him again and then he'd spend another three days working on something else.

'I said to him, "What are those speakers for?" and he explained that you sit on this crap stool and, as far as he was concerned, these speakers were the pinnacle of what you needed to hear a record on to make it right. Even more bizarre, the company who made these speakers found they had a fault which meant they only lasted a year before they blew up. Unfortunately, this company had gone out of business so Jim bought all the speakers they had left and kept them in his studio as prized possessions. He would sit and listen to a thirty-second section for four or five hours on his own through those speakers.'

By now, all eyes were on the band's third studio album – which featured Robbie on the cover as the artwork and project had been completed before he'd left – to see if Take That were about to implode. Against all odds, the record, called *Nobody Else*, was an absolute corker.

The band worked in a disciplined manner, starting at a sprightly 9 a.m. and working through until mid-afternoon, with the bulk of the recording taking place in Gary's home studio. The choice of location affected Gary's muse and he openly said that his parents had inspired many of the lyrics and moods on the record.

Released in late August 1995, just over a month after Robbie's departure, *Nobody Else* came as a huge sigh of relief for the anxious Take That fans who had waited nearly a year and a half for a new album from the boys. The album presented Take That as a mature act, Barlow as an established songwriter of some weight, and each individual member as an established star in his own right. The entertaining cover artwork mixed two iconic portraits by great artists of two different eras – the pop art of Peter Blake on The Beatles' album *Sergeant Pepper's Lonely Hearts Club Band* and 'The Arnolfini Marriage', a famous painting from the sixteenth century by Flemish painter Jan van Eyck that hangs in London's National Gallery.

Having made a few Beatles comparisons already, it seems only fitting that the artwork for the band's third studio album aped in many ways that classic *Sergeant Pepper* image for the Fab Four's seminal 1967 album. The sleeve art and packaging of the *Sergeant Pepper* album revolutionized the genre and helped establish the pop medium as art. Conceived by Robert Fraser, a London art dealer and friend of The Beatles, the project was the first to commission a fine artist to design an album cover for a rock group. Iconic pop artist Peter Blake produced a series of seventy or so cardboard, life-size cut-outs, along with waxwork dummies, to surround the Fab Four, who themselves chose the characters to be involved. Writers such as William Burroughs and Oscar Wilde shared the stage with film stars including Laurel and Hardy and Marilyn Monroe. Boxer Sonny Liston was joined by Einstein, Gandhi and Bob Dylan. It was a cornucopia, a collection of the names who had either defined or influenced the band and, by definition, the age. As well as the astounding range of images, the sleeve was also the first pop album to include the lyrics to every song, and even contained a cardboard Sergeant Pepper moustache, along with other little extras. The package set a benchmark for pop and rock. For two decades – until the CD format almost killed the art-form – album design was as much an opportunity for creatives as any traditional gallery. And it all started with *Sergeant Pepper*.

Not to be beaten, Take That's cover for *Nobody Else* was similarly loaded with ephemera, which of course caused heated debate among the fan base as to its meaning and significance. Among the items on the sleeve were: plastic puppets of the band taken from their merchandise range, a tiny circular mirror containing a photo of the actual line-up, a Buddha, three clowns, a plastic bracelet, a silver dol-

phin from a lucky charm bracelet, a miniature Tetley Tea man, a Sherbet Dip, a mini Dalek toothbrush holder, cascades of flowers, a book entitled *The Art of Wisdom*, various dice spelling out the band's name, a picture of Elvis in his white outfit, toy cars, two kissing pigs, a sea-shell necklace, a Plasticine snail, some Far Eastern mini statues and a spinning top.

The artist brought in to create this odd mini-masterpiece was called Morgan Penn, who had famously created TV car adverts and a promo clip for Channel 4. He said that the band were very reluctant to be on the album cover in person, hence the dolls (often a sign of inner tension – the Spice Girls were not in their final video before Geri Halliwell left; instead they were represented by cartoons). Penn visualized a Take That altar and smothered this with items personally chosen by the band. Take That mailed him a box filled with odd little items, which he then arranged around the five dolls. Mark even sent him a list explaining why they had chosen each item.

The plastic bracelet actually belonged to Adam Ant, which he'd given to them after they'd met in a studio and announced he was a fan; the book was one of Mark's favourite reads; the photo of the band in the mirror is complete with a Port Vale FC mascot; and the Sherbet Dip was listed in their official annual as a favourite Gary Barlow pick-me-up.

As a footnote, the same album cover was released over a month after the UK version in the US and the cover artwork showed Take That as a four-piece.

'Sure' and 'Back for Good' provided stunningly good openers for the new album itself. That the second track came towards the closing chapters of Take That's story as a fivesome was even more appropriate – the irony of the lyric not lost on the Robbie fans. 'Every Guy' kept the mood reflective, but brought the tempo up again. Funky beats and hip-hop accents throughout reminded everyone that Take That were nothing if they were not Britain's best contemporary soul band. 'Sunday to Saturday' was back in club-land, part Hall & Oates, part Bee Gees, with a clever lyric, dancing sax break and a rootsy vocal from Gary. On 'Nobody Else' Gary stepped back into reflective singer-songwriter mode, a gentle ballad with a slow-dance feel and hints of Americana in the lyric that peers into the lives of school-day lovers growing older together – he dedicated this song to his parents.

The album's third No. 1 hit was 'Never Forget' – like 'Back for Good' it was a song loaded with retrospective irony regarding the year ahead, but at the time Gary's lyric seemed to many listeners to be preparing the way for some big change in the band's future. It was loaded with messages for fans that few could misinterpret. 'Hanging On to Your Love', the next track, was back into Gary's favoured piano-soul love-song songbook, combining break beats with soft-shoe string arrangements and the by-now trademark Take That backing vocals. Gary's melodies – on album tracks as well as the best-known singles – were always timeless, but the contemporary arrangements made them irresistible. This was never more evident than on 'Holding Back the Tears' (not to be confused with Simply Red's 'Holding Back the Years' of a decade or so earlier). The track has a gorgeous melody and a wonderful arrangement, but it is very much a song of the mid-Nineties, an anthem for a million Take That fans to hang their memories on as they grew up themselves and worked their way through their own early romances. The dreamy arpeggio on the harp – the closing note of the song – says it all.

'Hate It' is funky bass and vocals, Gary with his soul hat on again, with call-and-response backing vocals and heavy bass drum beats to remind the family downstairs what the fans were listening to. Rapping Robbie introduced 'Lady Tonight' with his best Potteries patter running throughout the opening bars of the pumped-up tune and coming back later in the song. It's Robbie's most distinctive recorded rap on a Take That record to date, and was a neatly hidden signpost of solo things to come. This was another great melody, but more upbeat as the album came to a close, and Take That could almost have made the soundtrack for *Saturday Night Fever* on this song, their sound blending so many Seventies and Eighties soul icons, in particular Tavares, while the vocal backing is awash with Bee Gees influence.

Like its predecessor *Everything Changes*, *Nobody Else* ends not on an upbeat dance classic but on a reflective, moody song, 'Day After Tomorrow'. If a generation of young pop fans learned all about love from Take That songs, then Gary's lyrics made the sometimes difficult journey as easy as possible. 'Day After Tomorrow' smooches along beautifully, with choir-like vocals and an understated arrangement to the piano, bass and drums configuration. It closes down the album – and Take That's series of three unforgettable, original albums – quietly, sensitively, and with a pop dignity that two years previously might have seemed unlikely.

Naturally, *Nobody Else* was a massive No. 1 hit album despite the splintering of the original line-up, and among its eleven tracks were three No. 1 hit singles. In hindsight, however, it is interesting to note that life sales for the third album fall below half a million copies, almost 800,000 less than sales for the second album, *Everything Changes*.

Ben Ofoedu is most famous for his role as lead singer in Phats & Small, as well as his more recent acclaimed new project Four Story, but back in the mid-Nineties he supported Take That on their final arena shows. Chatting with him in an exclusive interview for this book about his experiences gives a fascinating insight into life on the road with Take That, their habits, their personalities and the sheer scale of their fame – as well as the atmosphere within the band a few weeks after Robbie left.

'It all started back in 1993. Take That were doing amazing things and I was in an aspiring boy band at the time. We were a bit hip hop, a bit R&B, a bit soul, and went by the name of Benz. We went to RCA and met Nick Raymonde, who signed us. We were very excited by that because, in theory, we were Nick Raymonde's next big discovery.

'As part of signing to RCA, they took us to a Take That concert – this was November 1993 – and the first thing I thought was how incredibly energetic the show was. Even though we were in a good boy band, I couldn't imagine how we would ever get to that standard. I was totally flabbergasted, to be honest – the high energy, the sheer entertainment value. The performance was amazing, a constant barrage of great songs, it was really astonishing. I don't think I have seen a show as good as Take That to this day. They were known for their shows, it was like a circus, you had to be there to experience it. The only show that was close to it, in my opinion, was MC Hammer, funnily enough, but although he had that same energy he used twenty dancers, whereas this was just five lads. I remember thinking they were quite big lads too – I'd only ever seen them on TV before and I was surprised how big they were – and this added to it all. There were three six-footers and this made the energy that much more dynamic. They were mastering major dance routines, there was so much power and energy. That was my first memory of Take That.'

Knowing this was what the band had achieved only eighteen months after they were nearly dropped was an inspiration to Ben and his group: 'This was an amazing chance to launch Benz, and it was an absolute honour for us because of what Take That had already achieved. We admired them greatly and looked up to their work rate especially. They had broken down a lot of doors for people like us, so it was a very exciting time.'

'I'M NOT SURE THERE WILL EVER BE A BAND THAT CAPTURED THE NATION'S HEARTS LIKE THEY DID.'

At the same time, the up-close reality of Take That's day-to-day lives was an eye-opener for Ben: 'From what I saw of their lives, it wasn't that easy. I heard stories through their press officer and marketing team that girls would scream, but guys had got a habit of hurling stones at them. There was a lot of jealousy, but stoning people is serious stuff. They had a very organized security team to deal with this, a great team. James and Paul, their two key security men, were integral to the team, they were interlinked with Take That. Also, they both looked very cool and that became almost a part of the image of the band too, these really cool security guys who were very professional, looked good, and well-liked by everyone within the business.

'One of the first things that happened after signing was that we were asked to support Take That on this massive arena tour. Apparently Take That were shown a load of videos and one of them was us performing in Derby. They saw this and said, "They're good. Let's have them on the tour!" It was such a buzz when we heard the news.

'But then, about four weeks or so before the tour, there was a rumour going round the circles around the band that Robbie had gone missing. So suddenly the tour was

up in the air and we were obviously devastated. We'd been looking forward to it so much, you can imagine … then suddenly it might all be off. For almost a full day behind the scenes, the tour was in jeopardy. I heard when I saw someone close to the band and they said, "Robbie's gone missing." I will always remember that moment. Then next thing I know, the tour is still going ahead but without Robbie. At that time it was very nerve-wracking, no one really knew how the tour was going to be received, but the reality was that the tickets were still selling and no one had brought them back for a refund, so it went on.'

Despite being involved in the music business, Ben freely admits he was star-struck when he first met the band in person: 'My first memory of Take That face to face was when we were trying to get into Manchester Nynex, but there were literally thousands and thousands of girls outside in the way. It was about four o'clock in the afternoon, we pulled up outside the backstage gate and there were thousands of fans. I'd never seen anything like it. The backstage doors slid open and we were ushered through and the first thing I saw was Jason Orange just the other side of the door in his boxer shorts sunbathing, sunglasses on, lying down. As the door opened, a couple of fans caught sight of him and they started screaming and security said, "Come on, Jase, come inside," which he did. To me he was a superstar, so to see him so close, face to face, it was a weird thing. Seeing them in real life was weird. Fame is an illusion, and in their case it was a good illusion.

'They were like superheroes at that point. I'm not sure there will ever be a band that captured the nation's hearts like they did. Bands since have sold more records, sure – the Spice Girls and so on – but I don't think it was the same, not for me anyway. People would talk about "our boys". They were nice northern lads from next door, the sort of guys mums would want their girls to fall in love with. While we were getting cabs around the tour venues, all the cabbies kept saying the same thing – that it was just like the Beatlemania. I don't think that was an exaggeration. Absolute mania, hysteria.'

The old adage that you should never meet your heroes is a good one, but Ben's first-hand experience of Take That merely confirmed what he had heard about them: 'I'd been told in the industry that they were pretty humble, but you don't believe that can be the case, not when you think how huge they were. Yet they were. The very first thing a member of Take That said to me was, "Hello, my name is Jason." Now, at this point everyone in the world who was into music knew every single member of Take That, yet he was humble enough to introduce himself like that. He didn't need to do that. I thought, *I know who you are. You're part of the most photographed band in the world!* Then he said, "Thanks for coming on tour with us. We saw your video and it was really good. I love your logo too, and I'm looking forward to seeing your show. Me and the boys are really into you." I was amazed. We were already in awe of it all, and then to hear that was incredible. Jason was just having a conversation with us but the confidence that gave to a new band coming through like us was incredible. We went away like "Wow!" He generated such excitement just from a little chat. That will always be a benchmark for me, the way Jason was that first time we met him.

'Then when we sound-checked on the first night Mark came and watched us rehearsing and was giving us a thumbs up all the time, waving, making us feel good. Some shows, I'd be on stage and look across and see some of Take That or Nigel watching us through a gap in the curtain, clapping, enthusing about us. It was almost like we'd been introduced into their family – their road team was like a family, they had chosen this family very, very carefully and those within it were looked after. They certainly looked after us. They were so humble, and from that point on I have always noticed when any celebrity isn't humble, because there are so few who are bigger stars than Take That were and they did it, so I can't help thinking, *Why can't these other stars do it? If Take That can do it* … It was a very attractive thing and I always said if I ever got that big I would be the same.'

'HE WROTE POP SONGS YOU WOULD FALL IN LOVE WITH ALL THE TIME, HE WAS A MAJOR TALENT.'

Various Monty Python films such as *Life of Brian* were a favourite source of on-the-road amusement, plus countless games consoles, usually playing Super-Soccer. The band were still, despite all that they had been through, a gang. Ben recalls that, despite the camaraderie, it was clear just by watching Take That sound-check and hang out backstage who was the central force: 'Gary was the most focused, concentrating on the show. You could see him in sound-check thinking what needed to be done and how to do it. They all called him "the Guv'nor". He was clearly a very influential and important figure in that band and a very talented man. Technically he was amazing, he knew so much and never missed the ball; he sang every harmony correctly, played keyboards brilliantly, he wrote pop songs that you would fall in love with all the time, he was a major talent.

'We did twenty dates, including ten at Earls Court. They were brilliant shows, they really were. The band had got so big by that stage that their touring party couldn't really travel very easily, so they did these long stints in massive venues. The touring machine was a logistical beast but it was all organized with amazing precision too, quite a thing to see up close. It was so tight backstage, and what was striking was that

although it was a huge set-up, everyone seemed to know everyone else and there was a really good vibe there, all the way up to the top. Somehow it felt intimate despite the grand scale.

'You'd go to the loo and bump into one of them and then you'd notice that they had security with them – they each had to have a security man with them at all times. The problem was, these venues were huge and people could sneak in, they can get through a door that isn't being watched or whatever, there is always that chance they can get in. So the band needed protecting. It wasn't a pretentious thing, and given the chance the boys would obviously not have had so much security, but it was an absolute necessity. Yet they were so down to earth that you'd almost forget the sheer size of their fame. It was fascinating to be around.

'Those dates also confirmed for me that Nigel was one of the all-time great managers. The way he did Take That on the road was like watching a mastermind at work. He knew what people wanted and he delivered it. Yes, we could see backstage that he ran a very tight ship, but that was what was needed, and as the band got bigger it was a good thing that he was so precise. At times things seemed to be chaotic but when you looked again it was not, it was all run so professionally and so well. Everything was controlled, calculated. People forget the music business is exactly that – a business –

and as such there are people needed to run that business. Bands need a good manager. They are into their music and performing, but you get an operation like Take That and you need someone else to look after it all. No one did that better than Nigel.

'Backstage, Nigel was so well grounded too, he also made us feel very welcome. After one show early on in the tour, he came into our dressing room and said, "I think your show is amazing, but there is something you should do … I think you should say, 'We are really pleased to be in the tour and Take That invited us, and thanks.'" We thought, *That's weird, why say that?* But we took his advice and it lifted our show up into the skies, it was such a tip, it was like saying we were really cool and that Take That fans should love us too, it made that connection with their audience.'

Like many people, when I booked my tickets, Robbie Williams was still a member of Take That. By the time the shows came around, he was out. I went to one of the Earls Court shows and, according to the promoter I spoke to in the days beforehand, the venue could have been sold out several times over. That's nearly 20,000 bums on seats every night. The band even had difficulty finding enough available T-shirt factories in Britain to print the merchandise as fast as they were selling it.

Part of this mass appeal was the ability to cross several markets. Obviously Take That's pre-teen and teen fans were their staple record-buyers, but it is not always a

given that a teen band will enjoy fans who are in their twenties, and certainly not fans in their thirties or older too. Take That had this back in the Nineties (and even more so when they re-formed, more of which later). At the Earls Court show there were a majority of teenage girls, some very young ones with parents; but there were also a very sizeable number of young adults, many obviously on a date. In addition, there were office outings, girls' nights, and generally more adult ticket-holders. Combining all these together produced massive sales.

The dancing was quite remarkable. Jason and Howard are indeed both 'big six-footers' and seeing their acrobatics was amazing. Jason was always known as the fitness freak of the group, eating no red meat, choosing fish, chicken and vegetables instead, following very punishing fitness regimes and steering away from some of the less healthy lifestyle choices made by the other band members. However, Howard wasn't far behind.

There was such a dramatic stage show, so many pyrotechnics, costumes, dancers, lighting, it was incredible. Yet I couldn't help but wonder what the atmosphere was actually like backstage. After all, Robbie had just gone, they were down to a four-piece for the first time, surely it must have been pretty fragile? Not according to Ben: 'They were all laughing, hanging out with each other, the atmosphere was very jovial. They were always cracking jokes and I didn't see any tension at all, I have to say. Backstage the morale was pretty good.'

The behind-the-scenes partying was not particularly evident, although this was not because of any apparent tension in the camp: 'They didn't party after shows,' says Ben. 'They'd done all that. They essentially did their job and then went home, especially for the Manchester shows. It was a very, very civilized environment. We had one party, the end-of-tour party, and that was fun. No one knew how the tour was going to go, but within a few nights it was obvious that it was going to be brilliant. The band themselves seemed to get on very well and knew when to have a laugh and when to knuckle down. They were seasoned pros, after all, by this stage. They went out there and did the business – they'd said they were going to do the tour, and despite Robbie leaving, they did it.'

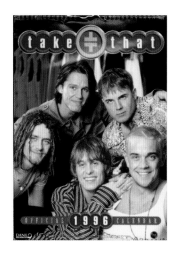

GONE FOR GOOD?

JUST OVER SIX MONTHS AFTER Robbie Williams left the band, the *Sun* newspaper's Andy Coulson reported that the remaining four members of Take That were planning to call it a day. At first, many people dismissed this as idle tabloid speculation, a theory reinforced by Nigel Martin-Smith's angry reaction. As that fateful day unfolded, however, RCA were contacted by pretty much every newspaper in the country and in Europe, and replied to the question of the band's future by saying that, although they were not sure of the plans for the long term, they were sure there'd be no split in the short term.

'THOUSANDS OF TEENAGE FANS HOMED IN ON THE PRESS CALL.'

Then, late in the afternoon, a press call was sent out saying the band was going to make a statement the very next day, 13 February (coincidentally Robbie Williams's twenty-second birthday). It may be hard to imagine the scale of this announcement in the context of more contemporary pop music, but everyone wanted to be there and anyone with even a vaguely passing interest in music knew about it. Schools across Britain reported hundreds of girls absent without leave as thousands of teenage fans homed in on the press call. Sky News ran a special report and streamed the press conference live with comments from expert observers.

'Unfortunately the rumours are true,' said Gary as soon as the foursome sat down in front of the massed ranks of the world's press. '"How Deep is Your Love?" is going to be our last single together and the *Greatest Hits* is going to be the last album, and from today … there is no more.'

You could almost hear the shockwaves reverberate around the UK like an earth tremor. It later transpired that the band had indeed planned to announce the split a week later at the Brit Awards, but the *Sun*'s scoop had hastened the need for a press call. Amazingly, Take That even said that just before they'd walked out to declare the band was over they took a moment together to make sure they were certain of what they were doing. It became apparent that they had enjoyed the Christmas break with their families and reconvened with a New Year's meeting, at which it was generally agreed that it was time for Take That to call it a day.

The sound bite everybody kept using was the opening quote from Gary saying, 'from today, there is no more'. On the radio, the way he said the words 'no more' sounded like he'd actually broken down crying. He hadn't. He was just affectionately playing with the crowd.

After Gary's opening and devastating gambit, in classic Mark Owen fashion, 'the Angel' tried to get the Q&A session going by simply saying, 'Well, there you go then …' Among the various lengthy and well-humoured replies to questions from the press were such brutally honest answers as this from Mark when reminded they'd said they'd never split up unless the fans lost interest: 'We do care very much about our fans …

there's been a number of factors that have made us change. We've done all that we can do as Take That, we took it to a level well beyond any of our expectations and, I suppose, beyond many of your expectations … basically we just want to reassure the fans that it isn't the end.' Yet there was clearly a large degree of backstage politics going on that would remain unseen: 'There have been a number of other factors which we don't really want to go into, but I'm sure you know what's going on behind the scenes.'

Mark had the gathered press in stitches with quips such as this: 'Howard's doing a *Playboy* set, he's been offered a few quid for that, and I've asked me mum to get me a job at Park Cakes. You don't need many qualifications for that so I'm lucky there, and "ex-pop star" is one of the qualifications that might get me in there. I've got a good vibe with the manager at Park Cakes and

I've got an interview on Friday actually, so I hope you'll all wish me well!' The biggest laugh of the day was reserved for his answer to the question, 'What about your solo career, Mark?' to which he replied, 'I haven't got one yet.'

'FROM TODAY …
THERE IS NO MORE.'

The quietly spoken Howard kept a back seat, but did say this: 'While I'm very emotional at the moment [just how emotional would become apparent several years later], I know that it's the best time now to finish at the top. We've always said that we would finish on top and it's very good for our careers ahead of us, so I think we're making the right move.'

Jason was equally quiet but did say this: 'We're all, quite naturally, going to have apprehensions about this but we're trying to look at it all positively and I think it's important for us all. We don't want any negativity. It was a very positive thing when we set out. We've achieved all that we set out to achieve – well, more – and now it's brilliant because we've got a new lifestyle, where we feature as individuals, and we're trying to look at it positively.'

Finally, denying that the real reason they broke up was Robbie's departure, Jason said, 'The main reason we've broken up is because we wanted to. We thought it was time, but we can't deny that there's been other pressures from other areas but we'd prefer not to make that a major issue here. It's a personal issue and we want to remain professional.' (A decade later, Mark Owen would say it was never the same after Robbie left.) Both Mark and Gary said they would be working on solo material, although Jason and Howard did not mention what their future plans were. Notably, Gary did not rule out the possibility of the band re-forming at some point in the future.

The immediate aftermath of the band's split was really quite remarkable. Every newspaper carried page after page on the event, evening news bulletins on television headlined with the split and radio stations all over the country ran day-long phone-ins and discussions. Worse still, the Samaritans did indeed have to set up hundreds of extra lines to cope with the torrent of calls from distressed fans, eventually offering a special hotline to cope with demand. It is not an urban myth; there really was some kind of mass hysteria when the band called it a day – a teenage girl's grief on a national scale. There were numerous reports of threatened suicides and one confirmed death in Germany.

Gary later acknowledged the difficulties the band had in keeping the same focus: 'There were such broad opinions of where we wanted to go next. We each wanted different things. The reason we all joined the group in the first place was we had weak elements in our characters: where someone else was strong, I was weak, and so on.'

Despite what he had said about going out at the top and understanding it was time to call it a day, in the ITV1 documentary in late 2005, *Take That – For the Record*, Howard made a shocking admission: he said he was so gutted by the split that he walked

down to the River Thames and actually thought about killing himself, but that he was 'too much of a shitbag to do it'. When Nigel Martin-Smith was told this in his interview he looked genuinely shocked and appalled and called it 'terrible'.

One final press-conference detail had been to announce that the band's final single, a cover of their fellow Mancunian Bee Gees track 'How Deep is Your Love?', would be released on 9 March 1996 (twenty years after the original). The video for this track was decidedly spooky, with all four being tied to chairs by a *femme fatale* and dangled over a cliff's edge before being sent plunging to their apparent deaths. Although record-company statements suggested this was recorded before the split was announced and was merely a coincidence, you couldn't but help draw some analogy with the band's career crashing to a halt. It was easily Take That's darkest moment on film, to coincide with their darkest hour as a group. The track was ordinary, and it seems a shame that this was the band's last outing as a single back then. 'Never Forget' would have made for a much more fitting finale, lyrically, musically and with the retrospective video.

Not surprisingly, however, on 3 March 1996 'How Deep is Your Love?' entered the UK charts at No. 1, where it stayed for three weeks, spending a further eleven weeks

in the charts on its way to sales of over half a million – their third biggest-selling single at that point, behind 'Babe' and the clear winner 'Back for Good'.

A month later, the record stores geared up for another stampede when the band released their *Greatest Hits* package. Advance orders were astronomically high, with the record eventually passing the magic million mark. Despite their split, Take That's last two releases proved that few bands could compete with them in terms of both their mass appeal and commercial might. The pop world had suffered a major fatality and millions of fans worldwide went into mourning.

Although no other boy bands of the time could touch Take That for popularity, almost within hours of the band announcing their split there was a feeling that a few young pretenders were jostling to grasp their crown. East 17 were themselves heading towards an untimely split, while the lesser-known Upside Down never made any real dent in the charts (and never hit the Top Ten). However, the band that seemed to fill Take That's footsteps seamlessly was the Irish quintet Boyzone – in fact, they would eventually enjoy more chart hits than Take That (sixteen) and more No. 1s too, with six to Take That's four.

'THE POP WORLD HAD
SUFFERED A MAJOR FATALITY.'

Shane Lynch of Boyzone has a lot of respect for Take That and freely admits that the band were a direct inspiration for Boyzone, as well as a key motivating factor for him to get into his own Irish group. His views on and experiences of the 'That-ers', as the group's members were nicknamed, gives a unique perspective on the influence and impact Gary Barlow's band had already had on the greater musical landscape. Even at the moment of their splitting up, observers such as Shane and his contemporaries were acknowledging their importance, as he told the author for this book:

'The first time I heard of Take That I was 16 and in my girlfriend's kitchen. On the fridge was a load of magnets of Take That and she was chattering away, going, "Oh, I really like him, and oh, I like him …" Obviously the jealousy set in immediately because she was talking about some other fella, you know. I wasn't really into music at the time other than a bit of hip hop but straight away she'd put my back up so my immediate reaction was, "Yeah, yeah, they're all gay!" That was the first thing that came out of my mouth, I was so jealous of somebody stepping on my territory, even though they were a pop band! My girlfriend liked them so I disliked them instantly.

'I was a mechanic at the time. I'd got kicked out of school the year before that and I was working for my father and I thought that was what my life was going to be, a mechanic. I wasn't into music and entertaining people and singing and dancing, I didn't go to stage school, I didn't do none of that kind of stuff. Then a school friend of mine called Mark Walton who I'd not seen for quite some years just knocked at my door and said, "All right, Shane. I haven't seen you for a couple years but, listen, I just wanted to ask you, are you interested in being in a band?" They way he put it was, "We're good-looking fellas and I wanna do a bit of singing, a bit of dancing like that band Take That." When I heard them mentioned I said, "Yeah, I know them fuckers … yeah, I'll be in your band."'

Shane's life was about to change beyond recognition, just like Take That's had that day they met Nigel Martin-Smith. 'Mark said, "I've got this name of this guy called Louis Walsh and he's a manager." So I went to me father and I said, "Listen,

Dad, can I have Friday morning off? I'm going to be in a band." He said, "Well, can you sing?" and I said, "No," and he said, "Can you play an instrument?" and I said, "No." So he said, "As long as you are back by two o'clock then." I knew I couldn't do all that, but Take That were such a motivating force.

'We went to see Louis Walsh and the basic breakdown of it all was, "Look, we want to put a band together just like Take That." It was deliberately targeted to be like them, although obviously the Irish version. Just like Take That, an advert was put in the national press looking for the rest of the band and articles were written very quickly saying, "These two fellas are the next Take That …" We even went to see Take That play in Dublin and some girls asked for our autographs because they'd seen us in the papers. It was quite funny.'

'WE ADMIRED TAKE THAT BECAUSE THAT WAS WHO WE WANTED TO BE.'

Although Boyzone were quickly up and running, they didn't enjoy their first UK chart hit until December 1994 with 'Love Me for a Reason'. They were well known on the pop circuit by then, however, and were invited to attend the *Smash Hits* Poll Winners' Party that Christmas, where Take That (still a five-piece at this point) were also per-forming. 'That was the first time we actually got to meet Take That,' recalls Shane. 'By then, the press had created rivalry between us – you know, we're fighting for their crown. That moment when we saw them sitting there, it was like, "Shit, Take That are here, we are just newcomers … what's going to happen?" Obviously we'd been put on the same pedestal as them and I guess it wasn't nice for them because it was these Irish boys coming in to challenge their supremacy.

'We had no ill feeling towards them whatsoever. We admired Take That because that was who we wanted to be. We never felt anything against them. The press did that for us. We went over to meet them and said "Hello". We didn't know if we were going out

to a bit of a row, a bit of hostility, but still we wanted to go and shake their hands because that's who we wanted to be, we wanted to be them.

'I tell you what, all the lads are really, really spot on. Gary was the only one who was ever so slightly stand-offish. I remember people talking about Gary being a little bit funny about it, but, to be fair to him, the next time we bumped into him he was absolutely fine. Mark was the stand-out character for me really, because he was so idolized by women at the time. He was lovely too, the most friendly, the nicest fella. We made no secret of our admiration, telling them, "It's good to meet you. I don't know what all the press have been saying but we think you're amazing and all we want to do is be like you."'

Boyzone only had two chart hits before Robbie left Take That, but they were already very high profile and their success was gathering momentum. The two bands' paths rarely crossed, even though they were both doing the same promotional and live circuits around Europe. For now, Take That were the undisputed kings. 'I saw them live,' says Shane with disarming honesty, 'and thought, *How am I ever going to be able to do that?* That's what I thought, that's the truth. Like I said, I was just a mechanic and all of a sudden I'm in this concert and I'm looking at this amazing band who we were aspiring to be. It's just pure madness. But you know, I kept my head down and blagged my way through it.'

Shane is also boldly honest about Boyzone being pleased when they heard Take That had split up: 'Oh, listen, without telling a lie, we were delighted, absolutely. Our biggest rivals were breaking up, too right! Not in a bad way or personally, because we liked them all, but in a purely professional sense. Business is business at the end of the day.

'At one awards ceremony, Gary actually handed a crown to us and said words to the effect of, "We hand this crown over to Boyzone," or something like that. That was nice in one way, but at the time we were also kind of thinking, *You didn't need to say that because we were gonna take it anyway!* We probably never would have actually, we were just being cocky really. But that aside, it was a good moment when he actually came out and said that.

'Take That are a big part of Boyzone's history, the same way New Kids were for Take That, you know, and even Bros had a big part to play in the family tree before that. For me, out of all of those bands, Take That were definitely the biggest. Even though later bands sold more records and had more hits, Take That were the biggest.'

An appearance at the Brit Awards in February preceded Take That's final tour, with what at the time was considered to be their last ever gig being in Amsterdam on 5 April 1996.

For Take That, for now, it was all over.

DON'T LET THE STARS GET IN YOUR EYES

'I THINK I WAS IN CANADA when I got the call that Robbie had left the band,' recalls Nick Raymonde, Take That's A&R man throughout their career. 'I said, "Just tell him, whatever record he wants to make, I will make a great record with him." The record-company colleague on the other end of the phone said he wasn't sure Robbie would stay on the label and I said, "I don't even want to think about that possibility."'

'WHATEVER RECORD HE
WANTS TO MAKE, I WILL MAKE
A GREAT RECORD WITH HIM.'

A couple of weeks after Robbie left Take That, he was due to appear on Channel 4's *Big Breakfast* as a guest presenter (reportedly being paid £2,000 a day to do so). At the time the show was the lone bastion of alternative thinking in morning schedules dominated by water-skiing dogs and agony aunts. Suitably encouraged by my wife, we trekked down to the East End canal-side location of the *Big Breakfast* house to see him turn up, assuming there'd be a few dozen people with the same idea. After all, he'd not yet released anything. There were over a thousand people already waiting when we arrived at 6 a.m.

At the end of his stint, Channel 4 confirmed that viewing figures were up 600,000 per day while Robbie was on screen. It was obvious at that moment that the British public already had an acute fascination with Robbie Williams. After what seemed like an eternity, a door opened at the side of the house and Robbie, this pop peacock, strutted down a small paved path towards the fences holding back these hysterical girls. And gay men. And me.

He stopped about twenty feet short of the fence and just smiled, laughed and said 'Hello'. He shook a few hands and kissed a few bright-red faces, before heading back into the house for his interview. His 'presence', his 'X factor' for want of a better word, was quite shocking. Your eyes were quite literally on stalks. He's much taller than you expect, over six foot; and he's better looking than you expect – in the flesh he is really quite striking, it looks like someone is shining a torch through the back of his head and out into the world through his startlingly green eyes. At this point he was not 'the country's favourite entertainer', this was pre-*I've Been Expecting You*, pre-Knebworth, pretty much pre anything of note. None of which seemed to matter. On that cold, damp East End morning, surrounded by bleary eyes and shivering shoulders, Robbie Williams was just obviously a *star*.

The following February, how did Robbie Williams react to the birthday news that his former band-mates had called it a day? 'To be honest, I'm more worried about whether Port Vale will win their match tonight.' Robbie's beloved footy team did win. They triumphed 2–1 against Everton in the FA Cup.

At first, the underdog would beat the bookies' favourite. Just like Port Vale … but there would be a twist in the tail …

'ROBBIE WILLIAMS WAS JUST OBVIOUSLY A *STAR*.'

In August 2003 Robbie Williams was to play two nights at his own headline Knebworth show in front of 250,000 people, confirming his status as the country's premier solo artist, as well as his place among pop's super-rich. Yet exactly seven years earlier to the month he was facing potential financial disaster, battling personal issues and struggling to establish a solo career. Rarely has there been such a phoenix-like return to form.

While his former band-mates were releasing and touring Take That's final studio album, Robbie Williams was enduring a hellish twelve months or so. On the surface it was all about partying, laughing in interviews, being seen out on the town with famous faces. Behind all this was a court case that threatened financial ruin, contractual issues with his record company and spiralling personal problems. All was not well within the Robbie Williams camp.

Before Robbie could even contemplate a solo career, he had to extricate himself from the contract with RCA that had been signed during his Take That years. Usually there are conditions applied to prevent members leaving and costing a record company lost

revenues and so on. After lengthy and expensive legal arguments – Robbie told one reporter it cost him £400,000 in legal fees, and a figure of at least £250,000 was also mentioned – a confidential resolution was reached that freed him up to sign with another record company. Shortly after a resolution was reached, Robbie commented, 'It was never about money, it was about freedom. Money's horrible – the root of all evil. It gets in the way. It cocks up relationships and takes away people's souls. I don't have lots of it now and losing it didn't bother me. I've been a millionaire twice, but I'm certainly not one any more.' Rumour suggested – although this was never shown to be true – that Robbie would not be allowed to release a single before Gary had first put out his own début solo track.

The company Robbie chose to sign with was Chrysalis, who, it must be said, were taking a sizeable risk. After all, at this stage there was no 'Angels', no Knebworth, merely a pile of lurid tabloid headlines and forthcoming High Court papers to peruse. Nonetheless, Robbie signed a £1.5 million three-album deal. The contract helped refuel Robbie's depleted finances, and more importantly gave him a clean break to re-launch his solo career.

However, his mind seemed to be focused on anything other than music. He seemed to be somewhat at sea. He filmed a lucrative advert for 7-Up soda, said to have earned him £100,000, but within a few months was admitting he'd regretted the move – not

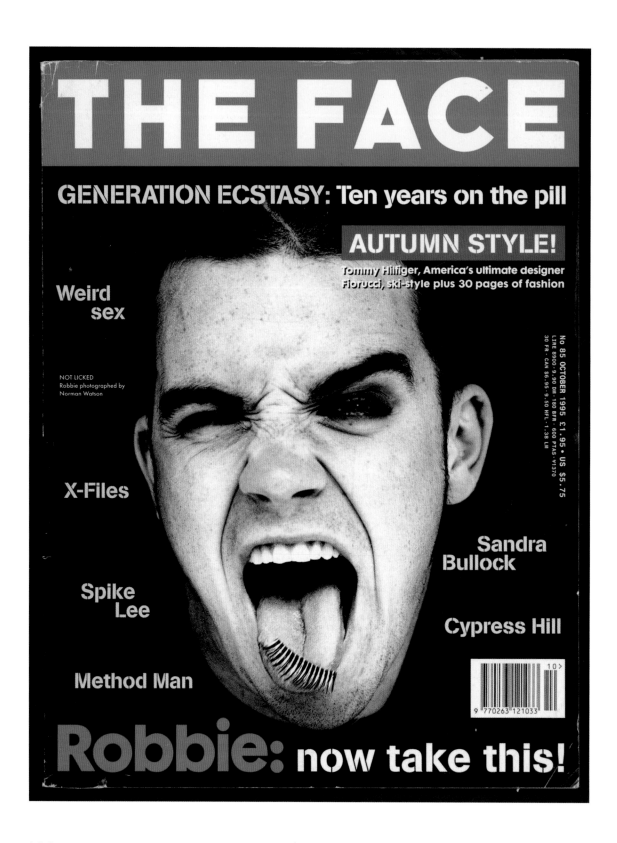

THE FACE

GENERATION ECSTASY: Ten years on the pill

AUTUMN STYLE!

Tommy Hilfiger, America's ultimate designer
Fiorucci, ski-style plus 30 pages of fashion

**Weird
sex**

NOT LICKED
Robbie photographed by
Norman Watson

X-Files

**Sandra
Bullock**

**Spike
Lee**

Cypress Hill

Method Man

No. 85 OCTOBER 1995 · £1.95 · US $5.75
LIRE 8900 · 9.90 DM · 180 BFR · 600 PTAS · ¥1370
30 FR · CAN $6.95 · 9.50 HFL · 1.38 LM

9 770263 121033   10>

Robbie: now take this!

least because he was photographed in a blond wig, stilettos and knickers. 'I got giddy with my freedom and when those [7-Up] pictures came out I left the country because I hated what I'd done. Now I'm working, I won't be carrying on like that. I'm bored with being pissed. I'm bored with being fat and I'm really bored with depression.'

Robbie's weight was ballooning. He joked about 'eating all the pies' and he certainly looked that way. Back in the October of 1995 Robbie famously did a front-cover feature in fashion bible *The Face*, his first interview since his departure from the band.

In retrospect, we now know that he was in the middle of his most difficult year; nonetheless, it made for compelling reading. Indicative of his weight issues, Robbie started the interview with a meal from McDonalds.

Seeing pictures of him during that phase, it is not surprising that he has admitted to struggling with his weight on occasion. While still in Take That, Robbie had once prophetically said, 'I like anything, but I worry about my weight, so every now and then I watch what I'm eating; otherwise, I could end up a fat waster.' His earliest memory, he told the press, was having the mickey taken out of him on a beach as a chubby 4 year old, so this issue was not new to him. 'I'll never be happy with the way I look. The only thing I really like about myself is my huge willy!'

The excess was matched by many now-famous insults about his former band members and ex-manager. The first time Robbie came face to face with his former band-mates was at the National Television Awards in August. While the others said nothing, Mark simply waved and said, 'Look after yourself.' Robbie was found to be very upset backstage afterwards – after all, Mark and Robbie had always been close friends so the encounter was particularly distressing.

Some of Robbie's most stinging side-swipes and, indeed, blatant insults have been reserved for Nigel Martin-Smith. In the actual sleeve notes for his début album, Robbie dedicated it to Nigel with the accompanying message, 'For Nigel. My past is something I find difficult to accept, especially the part with you in it.' Inevitably, while he was keen to talk about his forthcoming début solo album and the future, pretty much every interview with Robbie was dominated by questions about the split with Take That. The year or so after his own departure, and then in the months surrounding various solo careers, Robbie's regular lambasting of the band's members was frequent tabloid fodder, although the four band-mates maintained a dignified stance, which usually meant no comment was made in reply.

This obvious period of rebellion against the constriction of being in a tightly run boy band was painful to watch. Robbie once said, 'I would put a cigarette in my mouth and seven people would try to light it for me,' and yet here he was basically out on the piss without any entourage, just his mates. It was an odd contrast – from what he had once likened to a prison sentence to this new Wildean excess.

'I remember once taking a night out in Germany,' says Shane from Boyzone, speaking to me for this book about this period of Robbie's life. 'At our hotel there were the Spice Girls and Robbie and it was quite a good night, to say the least. We had a drink and a good time. Robbie at that point was all party, party, party, you know, just going out and having a laugh, enjoying himself. From my own experience, I think you really have to look around you, in front of you, behind you, left, right … if some of your friends are good people to be around, you will often end up like those friends.'

At times, Robbie seemed to be photographed falling out of every trendy London drinking hole, such as the Atlantic Bar and Grill, often with 'celebrity' mates like the Gallagher brothers. By contrast, during periods when Robbie had 'gone to ground', he was rarely spotted in London. Yet, oddly, on one occasion he was roaming the streets of a provincial Welsh town freely. Sarah Holcroft, a fan of the band, was living there at the time and, rather bizarrely, Robbie Williams was a regular face around town. 'It was definitely when he was hiding from the media,' she told me in an interview for this book. 'Owen Morris, who produced some stuff for Oasis, has a recording studio in Crickhowell and Robbie was hanging out there and staying at the famous Bear Hotel. He hung around the town for about three weeks – mostly on his own, wearing a black puffer jacket, looking quite sad. Some of the sixth-form lads reckoned he'd chat to them in the pub. Anyway, after about ten days of playing it cool, I decided it was time to stop walking past him and pretending I didn't know who he was, and went over and asked for his autograph. He was very nice and asked me what my name was and signed something for me.' Given that he has been accused of only being approachable if a paparazzi is within snapping distance, this friendly demeanour in the distant Welsh valleys can only be to Robbie's credit. Unfortunately, back in the smoke of the capital city life was about to become far from easy for the ex-Take That-er.

'THERE IS DEFINITELY GOING TO BE A LIVE SHOW, A LIVE ACT.'

On 6 August 1996 Take That's manager Nigel Martin-Smith issued a legal writ at the High Court claiming damages against his ex-client Robbie Williams, covering monies said to be owed from unpaid commissions while he was in Take That, as well as from Williams's advance for the band's final *Greatest Hits* compilation. Furthermore, there was a claim put in to court for a tiered percentage of Robbie's future earnings until 2006 (and this was all in addition to legal cases brought against Robbie by two former managers during his early solo career).

Former band-mates and managers facing each other across a courtroom is nothing new, but it was still headline news when Nigel Martin-Smith issued the proceedings. The problem with any band enjoying the success of the magnitude that Take That did is that there are very serious amounts of money involved and people expect that their share is fairly distributed. Ten million album sales and twenty million singles is one hell of a business. People felt entitled to their fair share of what was millions of pounds – in Take That's case, the figure of £17 million career earnings was thought to be a conservative estimate. However, music has always been the most incendiary of mediums, drawing in extroverts, eccentrics, artists and unusual char-

acters who do not live their lives by what the small print in a contract might say or what legal obligations they may have signed up for. The result is a perennial queue of former band members lining up outside the High Court in London, arguing with each other over royalties, managers chasing commission they insist is owed, various parties disputing ownership of band names and song copyrights and so on. For now, Robbie's legal team started to construct their strategy while the star himself turned his attention to the business of launching his solo career. In July 1995, a few days after leaving the band, all he said was, 'I'm just going to go away and write now. There is definitely going to be a live show, a live act, and I guarantee that will be quite an event, but when it's going to happen I don't know.'

The context for Take That's final split and Robbie Williams's attempts to go solo (and indeed Gary's and Mark's) was not entirely in the favour of former boy-band members. However, great pop bands can sometimes transcend musical fashion, and in part Take That were able to achieve this. Only a few baggy-trousered years before they were formed, their own emotional homeland of Manchester had spewed forth the last great British musical era of the Eighties, the so-called Madchester scene. The Mancunian corner of the music world once again provided a plethora of bands revolutionizing the rock and dance format – the Stone Roses led the way, with the Happy Mondays and Inspiral Carpets following closely behind, as 'baggy' music swept the nation up in a tide of flares, long-sleeved shirts and Joe Bloggs clothing.

Madchester, however, pre-dated Take That but seemed to have no effect on the popularity of the band once they began to break through in the early Nineties; but by the time Robbie left Take That it was only one month before the battle between Oasis and Blur for the No. 1 spot epitomized the peak (and some would say nadir) of so-called 'Britpop'. The first whiffs of this new movement came in 1993 with the early singles of a band called Suede, led by the enigmatic and inspirational Brett Anderson. Set against a backdrop of slacker-driven grunge culture, whereby American music and fashion had dominated the British alternative scene since 1991, Suede's songs talked of highly stylized, romantic London dramas, and Brett's peculiar camp Englishness carried it all off to perfection. Suede had swagger, style, and above all the songs – while Take That were releasing their début album, Suede were heralded by Melody Maker with an infamous front-page headline reading 'The Best New Band in Britain'. They did indeed change the face of British music – it was a million miles from grunge's tiring machismo and mainstream corporate feel.

'HE WAS TALKING UP SOLO MATERIAL THAT SOUNDED DISTINCTLY IN THIS GENRE.'

Britpop really started to blossom in 1993, boosted by Blur's pivotal second album, *Modern Life is Rubbish*, which openly paraded their Anglo-centric interests. With the fading recession and the sense of gloom that had made grunge seem so appropriate in the UK, the alternative kids began to look for something more uplifting. Not so Take That fans, who were busy buying 'Pray' and 'Relight My Fire' en masse. Nonetheless, the festivals that bands like Nirvana and Pearl Jam had revitalized were now taken over by a string of newly confident British bands – Blur, Suede, The Boo Radleys, Pulp and even a rejuvenated New Order.

The untimely death of Kurt Cobain and the arrival of Blur's third album *Parklife* sparked the deluge that would finally divert attentions away from sugary pop and grunge. Suddenly, there was a wash of superb British bands, with quirky albums and massive followings. In the next splendid eighteen months Pulp finally broke their fourteen-year duck without mainstream recognition and produced a sexually subversive, comical, seedy masterpiece in their first major-label album *His 'n' Hers*. Elastica, the Auteurs and the soon-to-be-global Radiohead also all made an impact. Supergrass's début album *I Should Coco* hit No. 1, and a litany of other bands enjoyed purple patches as well, including Shed Seven, Portishead, The Bluetones, Marion and Dodgy.

Unlike Take That, however, the international appeal of these bands was limited.

Oasis, the late-comers, took all the honours and enjoyed great worldwide success as well as a high-profile fan in Robbie Williams.

And the relevance of all this to Take That and Robbie's story? It's twofold: firstly, Robbie was seen as the bastard child of Britpop and teen pop, the rebel who had leapt out of the boy-band flames and into the hedonistic Britpop fire. He was mates (briefly) with the Gallaghers, he was seen hanging out backstage at gigs with many of Britpop's key proponents and he was talking up solo material that sounded distinctly in this genre. Secondly, Take That – and thus, by public perception, Gary Barlow – were starting to feel 'old hat', their soul-influenced feel-good pop music completely at odds with the quirky, Anglo-centric substance of so many of Britpop's hits. Their time in the spotlight had been called to a close by the band themselves, but with this backdrop it may have been approaching anyway. The question was, to what degree would the three former band-mates who had announced solo ambitions succeed in pursuing their respective careers?

OPEN ROADS, ENDLESS POSSIBILITIES

WHILE RUMOURS OF A TERMINAL Take That split had abounded, the hot topic was not if but when Gary Barlow would go solo and, more to the point, exactly how massive he would be. The generally accepted prediction was that he would become 'the new George Michael', and with good reason, because the parallels with the designer-bearded ex-Wham! frontman were startling. Both were working-class kids whose penchant for writing songs had made them multi-millionaires; both penned tracks considered to be classic at remarkably young ages – 'Careless Whisper' was written when George was only 17, 'A Million Love Songs' when Gary was just 16; both had fronted a phenomenally successful boy band and won awards for their songwriting; and both cited people like Elton John and other classic writers as key influences. Finally, they both had beards that looked like they'd been pebble-dashed on.

The signs of a solo career for Gary were there way back in Take That's heyday. He'd won Ivor Novellos, but the key to his future lay with 'Back for Good'. Although it was a band song, not a solo track (unlike 'Careless Whisper'), it was this undeniable classic that made people finally sit up and acknowledge Gary as an accomplished songwriter. So it was no surprise when news filtered through that he was immediately working on a solo record following Take That's disintegration. He was openly excited: 'This has been another beginning. The first phase of my career was with Take That and this is the second. I love the risk factor, changes, taking chances.'

The début solo record was quite a while coming, however. Gary was certainly not short of material, rumours suggesting he had fifty songs for consideration, which was in keeping with his prolific reputation. The reason for the delay was entirely positive. Gary had recorded the bulk of the album himself and was heading towards finalizing the record when he travelled to America for a show in Los Angeles. At the gig was the powerful music biz exec Clive Davis, head of Arista, who told Gary after the show that he was so impressed he wanted to step in and become more involved. Essentially he said Gary could work with whoever he wanted – and he meant whoever. Thus it was that Gary was teamed up with such industry legends as David Foster and Diane Warren (who penned Toni Braxton's global smash single 'Unbreak My Heart') and Madonna and Shep Pettibone (on the track 'Love Won't Wait'). The album he'd recorded thus far was virtually scrapped and work recommenced. 'It's ten times better than the stuff I'd done, so I'm glad I delayed it,' he said at the time. Eventually, only four tracks from the initial sessions remained. 'It was quite difficult for Gary, really,' recalls Nick Raymonde, who was still working at RCA when the début solo album was released, 'because they eventually made a great job out of the record, great production, but it wasn't easy to get there for some reason.'

With the album *Open Road* finally ready for release and seemingly with the eyes of the entire music industry on him, Gary was very upbeat about its chances. 'I'm standing in front of what will hopefully be a very long career, and I could take any one of many directions. It is a lyrical progression from Take That. This is the most positive and optimistic music that I have written – it's more about having things than losing them … I think audiences have missed seeing me perform on my own, no other band members, no other instruments, just a piano and a vocal. It's that raw performance – that is what it's all about for me.'

The first release was the single 'Forever Love' in July 1996, just over twelve weeks after Take That's last gig in Holland and almost precisely a year after Robbie had left. Gary's yearning vocal, the emotive piano and ascending chord sequence recalled Elton John or Lionel Richie at their best, and Gary's vocal was as accomplished as ever.

Songwriters' manager Stephen Budd told me about his high opinion of Gary: 'He is a good pop writer. He was very unafraid, he wasn't attached to being "cool" at all. When you heard his demos they were done on like a DX7, very basic cheesy sounds which most songwriters would steer away from like the plague, but he wasn't afraid of that. Sometimes that is the best thing.'

'Forever Love' was, with a certain inevitability, a natural for the No. 1 slot as a hungry public awaited the release of Gary's solo album. Its success was helped by the fact he looked very sharp in the video, almost chiselled, and certainly appearing as if he had raised his game to new heights. The sales of the song were huge (over 269,000) and it entered the chart straight at the top, remaining in the Top Forty for four months. Reviews were generally positive, although a few critics suggested it was a little bland.

His second single, 'Love Won't Wait' (a previously unreleased Madonna song), also hit the top spot in May 1997, and enjoyed a superb remix courtesy of Junior Vasquez, although it slipped out of the charts after just seven weeks. Nonetheless, in that time it had shifted nearly 200,000 copies.

GMTV's Michael Metcalf recalls the fan frenzy around Gary at this point: 'We were booked to run an interview with Gary Barlow on his own and we ended up going round to Gianni Versace's shop. However, there were so many girls outside they ended up getting forty police to keep the fans back. Gary was penned inside and we spent hours in there, but it was just absolutely brilliant, he was a consummate professional. While I was in the shop, I was obviously looking at the beautiful clothes and Gary would keep walking up to me and saying, "Do you like that? Would you wear it if I buy it for you?" He seemed very generous. He was really, really nice.'

It was around this time that Gary and Nigel Martin-Smith parted company. With his profile and track record, Gary wasn't without representation for long and signed with Simon Fuller, the man behind the Spice Girls, *Pop Idol* and also acting at the time for Annie Lennox and Cathy Dennis.

'IT'S THAT RAW PERFORMANCE – THAT IS WHAT IT'S ALL ABOUT FOR ME.'

With Gary looking towards breaking America, this was a clever choice as Fuller's track record suggested he knew how to make inroads into the US. However, it was quite a shock when he split from Fuller soon after and set up his own management company, GloBe Artists, with the help of a new manager, Kristina Kyriacou, who'd worked with Take That for the last few months the band were together.

With two consecutive solo No. 1s already under his belt, it was perhaps no surprise that Gary's début solo album also entered the chart at the top spot, going on to achieve near-platinum sales at the time of just under 300,000. Again, reviews were fair and generally positive, although once more some detractors said it was too middle-of-the-road. Gary performed in front of 100,000 people at Capital FM's 'Party in the Park' show in London's Hyde Park and enjoyed scores of sold-out solo dates.

There were encouraging signs at first in the US, where Arista were gleefully looking at George Michael sales figures and predicting great things for Gary. 'So Help Me Girl', a cover of a country and western song by Joe Diffie, stalled just one spot short of the UK Top Ten, but as his first solo release in America it was a No. 1 song in the US Adult Contemporary charts, one of many variations on the main *Billboard* Hot 100. In the latter listing the single reached No. 44, a modest but encouraging start. American TV also seemed to be taking to him, with a coveted spot on *The Rosie O'Donnell*

Show being among the high-profile television PR coups. Another coup was the powerful YTV network in Canada producing a TV special about him. Take That's fame meant he was also in huge demand for live shows all over the world, even as far afield as Brazil, and tickets for his European shows were sold out in minutes.

But then, suddenly, it stopped.

Why?

The answer is for various reasons, but key among them was a song released by his former band-mate and now-adversary Robbie Williams, called … 'Angels'.

In the rush to be the first to release solo material, Robbie had lost – RCA made sure that Gary was first out of the blocks – but he was not far behind. Yet tracing back the odd tale, the start of Robbie's solo career was far from plain sailing.

With typical fanfare, Robbie Williams called a press conference to announce the launch of his solo career at one minute past midnight on 26 June 1996. The event, perhaps not altogether surprisingly, was rammed with over 300 top journalists from across Europe. With camp melodrama, a large screen showed Big Ben approaching

the midnight hour before the video to Robbie's first solo single, a cover of the George Michael song 'Freedom', was played. Then, cometh the hour, cometh the man … walking like a chicken. Robbie took his seat, said 'Hello' and complained about the England football team being knocked out of Euro 96, before starting to field questions.

Among his choice answers and comments, Robbie said, 'I want to be seen and heard as an artist and also have a lot of fun along the way – I'm dying to get out of my local place.' He denied the rumours that he was pursuing a career as a TV presenter and fuelled rumours that Oasis's Noel Gallagher might write material for him, saying further that Oasis were his favourite band.

Hinting at the core frictions in Take That, he also took a not-veiled-at-all swipe at Nigel Martin-Smith: 'I'd like to meet up with the manager in a fork-lift truck, souped up to go about 150 miles per hour non-stop with no brakes! I didn't mean that, honest.'

'JASON'S GONNA MAKE A BRILLIANT PAINTER AND DECORATOR, I'M SURE!'

Interestingly, while many headlines carried the news that Robbie thought Gary's solo single was awful, here's what he actually said: 'To tell you the truth, it's like this – I'd love to say it's not my cup of tea but it's all right. But in fact it's awful! Hear me out, hear me out! It's not me slagging him off again, it's that I know what Gary is capable of and I've heard all his stuff he's got coming out and he's got tunes like "Back for Good" and more – I don't understand the record company or him releasing this song. But you know what, the next solo single's gonna be fantastic and Gary's gonna have a really good career, I'm sure of it.' Unfortunately, he reserved some acid comments for other former band-mates, saying, 'Jason's gonna make a brilliant painter and decorator, I'm sure!'

That Robbie chose to run with a cover-version for his first single was a very risky ploy. Robbie had actually bumped into George Michael shortly after he'd left the band and was eager to hear the latter's thoughts. 'We just chatted, and of course, if anybody's going to know what the dealings with record companies are like or leaving bands it's gonna be him, so whatever advice he gave would have been good. We were talking about music, football and fruit!' George Michael later said he'd heard Robbie's version and loved it.

Jokingly, Robbie had at one point suggested his first release should be a pseudo-cover called 'Sacked for Good'. On a more serious note, some observers thought his choice of song was a direct swipe at Gary Barlow, given that Gary had been touted almost universally as 'the next George Michael', but Robbie denied this vehemently, saying, '[The single's] a statement. It's more of a statement than a single, to tell you the truth. The statement is, "I'm free now to do whatever I want and to do whatever I choose!" I've had twelve months in the mire, if you like, which means I've experienced all lows, and I certainly know what lows feel like now.'

The haste with which Robbie's début single and video were recorded was a kick-back to the days when Take That seemed to be releasing a song a month. In fact, when

it came to recording the video clip in Miami for the single 'Freedom', Robbie's own vocal had not yet been recorded to lip-synch to, so he had to sing along to a playback of the original George Michael version. He was full of confidence despite this fairly major hindrance: 'Consummate professional has got nothing to do with it. Stick a camera in front of me and I can't help myself. I'm having a passionate love affair with the limelight. When I open the fridge door and the light comes on, I do a twenty-minute stand-up routine. I turn it on and I love it. I'm going to be the biggest star in the world!'

'I'M GOING TO BE THE BIGGEST
STAR IN THE WORLD!'

Robbie had been on a health kick in preparation for the shoot, losing a stone in weight and stopping drinking unless it was water. Even so, looking at the footage now, he still

seems a lot heavier than his rather more toned look of later years. On the sleeve artwork he is barely recognizable as the Robbie Williams of later years. Cheekily he added a line saying, 'Thank you for buying this single to celebrate Robbie Williams' "Freedom".'

The song received sizeable radio play and charted at No. 2, kept off the top spot by the Spice Girls' début smash 'Wannabe' (his opening single still sold over a quarter of a million copies, just 17,000 short of Gary's 'Forever Love'). Around the single's release, Robbie played to 50,000 people on Clapham Common for Capital Radio's

'Summer Music Jam' and the lively reaction was one of the very first signs that the public still held a great affection for the singer, despite his recent shambolic lifestyle. Elsewhere, despite – or perhaps because of – his rock-star excess, rumours abounded that he had been approached to play the part of Renton in the big-screen adaptation of Irvine Welsh's hit novel *Trainspotting*; later, he was said to have turned down the offer of a role in a movie with Harvey Keitel because he was so busy working on his début album.

People, it seemed, just liked Robbie Williams.

However, with the début-single campaign completed, Robbie showed no sign of slowing down. By the autumn and winter of 1996, via a recommendation from his friend Sir Elton John, he started to see celebrity psychologist Beechy Colclough, an Irishman famous for helping to straighten out the lives and minds of scores of big-name casualties of rock and roll. His treatment also later involved a six-week course at Clouds House in Wiltshire in June 1997, which Robbie likened to 'having your head cleaned for a bit'.

This involved no TV, magazines or books and a twelve-step programme originated in America. Oddly, given his fame, Robbie shared the facilities with numerous NHS patients. To his immense credit, Robbie has never shied away from talking about his treatment; indeed, he seems to almost welcome the chance to talk about it, and of course often makes self-deprecating jokes about such trials and tribulations. Of course, his turbulent private life has always made him ever more fascinating to the press and public alike.

'PEOPLE, IT SEEMED, JUST LIKED ROBBIE WILLIAMS.'

GMTV's Michael Metcalf interviewed Robbie during this period and recalls that it was obvious all was not well: 'We got an interview with Robbie in Barcelona where we spent a day with him. It was fairly obvious he'd been partying quite a bit. He managed to pull together enough, though, to be fair. Even though it was so early in his solo career, we were forced to do the interview in the grounds of the hotel because of the amount of fans outside. I have always really liked him – that part of playing the Artful Dodger back when he was a kid, he's still that cheeky chappy, you can't help but like him. For me, he comes across as a nice guy, but sometimes you feel like there's so much talent there and he just doesn't know where to go. Personally, I just felt bad after that Barcelona trip, because Robbie didn't seem happy at all.'

THE PHOENIX UNFOLDS

BY THE SPRING OF 1997 Robbie was finally looking a little more in control. He spoke to the press about having enjoyed his year of partying but how glad he was that it was over and he could concentrate on writing songs. Furthermore, with the solitary 'Freedom' single his only release to date, he even intimated that he partly wished he hadn't even put that out.

'I could have done with a whole year off, so that [in 1996] I could start afresh. When I released "Freedom" I was like returning to that world again and in some ways it was just too much. When you've been in something as intense as Take That you need enough time off afterwards to weigh everything up and sort out how you feel.' Indeed, without 'Freedom' on his forthcoming solo début album, the song is somewhat confined to a black hole in terms of Robbie's back-catalogue.

There were still darker days ahead. Robbie's court case with Nigel Martin-Smith reached its climax in the summer of 1997. With a solo career yet to really take off and with a potential bill in excess of £1 million, if he lost the case some observers suggested the star would be on the brink of the abyss. The papers knew that there would be much talk of Robbie's partying, but those expecting the singer to shuffle up to court looking dishevelled and out of control were disappointed. The spell in rehab had obviously had a huge impact. Robbie arrived in designer sunglasses, his hair smartly shaved into a grade-one crop, and clearly having lost a considerable amount of weight since the nadir of the 'I ate all the pies' days – supposedly two stone. If nothing else, Robbie's appearance and confidence in front of the media during the lengthy case showed the public that he was back on form. 'I feel fantastic, like a new man. I'm in good shape,' he told waiting reporters outside the court.

Inevitably, whereas a PR man may be able to hide tensions and deflect rumour, being under oath introduces a certain harsh reality to descriptions of events within an industry that is fuelled by exaggeration and gossip. In short, the tabloids in particular had a field day during the case, recounting in minute detail the quotes and accusations made by both sides.

Thus we heard from Martin-Smith's lawyer, Richard Millett, of Robbie's 'taste for glamorous and flamboyant company, alcohol and narcotics'. Furthermore, Robbie 'was turning up for work hung over and unable to rehearse' and 'he began to behave in a manner out of step and out of synchronization with the rest of the band'. He highlighted the band's understandable desire to maintain a clean-cut image, a perfectly reasonable strategy when marketing a boy band to young girls. 'They were supposed

to be the sort of boys girls could take home to their mum for tea,' he said in court. In addition, given the huge demands on a professional band's time and life, it was suggested Robbie had lost interest. Martin-Smith's lawyer said that Robbie's 'druggie attitude' had threatened a £2 million tour, and even when he did leave, Robbie had not given him the six months' notice he understood to be required, meaning that he was still owed six months' commission on Robbie's earnings. Martin-Smith denied he had sacked the star.

Robbie's lawyers, including the esteemed Michael Silverleaf, argued that the band's manager tore up the deal by dismissing him and therefore refuted the claims. He accused Martin-Smith of humiliating Robbie by raising Gary's complaints in front of other band members. Martin-Smith denied this, saying, 'All the band were paranoid and stressed out because they were at the top of the profession. I was just trying to give them a pep talk.' It was argued Martin-Smith was instrumental in telling the rest of the band to ask Robbie to leave – a fact denied by Martin-Smith – even though it was put forward that Robbie was prepared to fulfil commitments to the forthcoming tour. Martin-Smith had allegedly asked Gary and Jason to try and convince Robbie to stay in July 1995, but had said that if they couldn't, it was best if he left immediately. Robbie said that Martin-Smith therefore breached his duty to act in the best interests of all the members of the group. Robbie said he was summarily dismissed, while Martin-Smith said he was advised firing Robbie was 'not an option' and that he reluctantly decided that if Robbie wanted to go they should let him.

The rift with Gary was always going to be highlighted, and it was noted that Robbie refused to be 'one of Gary Barlow's backing singers'. Mark Owen was described as 'close to collapse' over the tensions within the band, while Gary and Jason were both named as wanting Robbie to leave. There had been plans to call them both to the witness stand but this never happened. It was reported in court that Mark and Howard were more 'laid back', and perhaps, the assumption must be made, were less involved in the confrontation. Robbie did not take the stand.

'I FEEL FANTASTIC, LIKE A NEW MAN.'

The case concluded in the last week of July 1997, by which time it almost felt like the bones of Take That had been picked over by the public and media alike. Every single court session saw the public gallery packed with teenage girls. Tabloid circulation figures were up, and everyone was fascinated by the case. Apart from Robbie, perhaps, who on one occasion after two hours of detailed legal arguments walked out of the court and said to the waiting press hordes, 'I don't even want to be here. I should be sunning myself in the park. But after this I'm going to become a member of the clergy. I'm serious. I'm off to India to become a priest.' He pointed out later that he was only joking and at another time said, 'I don't know what to make of all this. I can't believe this is all over money.'

After a long wait, Mr Justice Ferris finally delivered his decision in October 1997. Robbie was ordered to pay Nigel £90,000 immediately and asked for the star's earnings since leaving Take That. Robbie's appeal to the Court of Appeal was dismissed.

To this day, there appears to be a lasting and severe friction between the two former colleagues. On the ITV1 documentary Robbie was scathing and Nigel sounded bemused as to why Robbie was like this, saying, 'I gave him his career as far as I am concerned.' I think it is safe to say that there will not be a reconciliation between those two for some time to come.

The renaissance of Robbie Williams started when he first met future fellow songwriter Guy Chambers. At first, Robbie made out that he found writing songs easy and that he had accumulated a pile of tracks within a few months of leaving Take That. By 1997, however, he admitted this was, at best, an exaggeration. His choice of co-writer proved to be the catalyst for some of the nation's most memorable recent pop songs. Robbie's record company gave him a list of people he might like to work with and he picked Guy, not because he knew of him, but because 'it was a spiritual thing. It was like a voice inside my head telling me to pick him. And it's worked. It's dead weird really but I just knew his name sounded right.' Robbie attributes this strong inner sense to his mother, who he says reads Tarot. He has also spoken of moving house because of being unsettled by ghosts and even of tape machines turning themselves on and off.

Guy and Robbie hit on an immediate, productive and highly creative chemistry. The bulk of the album was completed in six days. By April 1997 Robbie was ready to unleash his second single, the first original Robbie composition, 'Old Before I Die'. The aptly titled début solo album *Life Thru a Lens* was released in September 1997 and met with warm, and in some cases rabid, reviews (the provisional title had been *The Show Off Must Go On*).

The packaging of *Life Thru a Lens* presented a fictionalized account of Robbie's hectic private, social and professional life, a pictorial ride through glamour models, paparazzi, the cheeky lad next door and the superstar with *those eyes*. The album immediately established Robbie as the coolest ex-Take That member. The opening track, 'Lazy Days', bore evidence of Rob's new-found interest in rock, with heavily strummed guitars and esoteric Beatles/Oasis-like swirling instrumentation. Robbie's voice was full and assured, freed from the multi-part harmonies of the Take That sound, the lyrics promising many delights among the ten tracks to follow.

The fizzy punk of 'Life Thru a Lens' itself kept the pace of the album up, a slice of celebrity life taken apart: rich daddies, fashions and passions changing by the minute, mummy picking up the pieces from the damage caused by cheques that bounce … and a wicked swipe at the inbreeding of the celebrity upper classes. 'Ego a Go-Go' levelled another series of punches at ivory-tower egos that Robbie had clashed with along the way, a bitter slap for unnamed characters from Robbie's past maybe?

If Gary had been the balladeer extraordinaire in Take That, then the fourth track on Robbie's solo début stopped listeners dead in their tracks. Co-written with songwriting partner Guy Chambers, 'Angels' burst the banks of pop and sent a message to everyone who had imagined there was only one great writer in Take That.

How to follow 'Angels'? Badly, in this case. 'South of the Border' kicks off with grungy grooves and more observational writing about the characters in orbit around Planet Robbie. The chorus is a mundane piece, Oasis-heavy with distorted guitar and snippets of conversational voice dubbed over the music. Fellow future single 'Old Before I Die' had a solid rock feel, Bryan Adams with the fun button turned up, with a fantastic, anthemic chorus. The acoustic strumming of 'One of God's Better People' slowed the pace of the album right down, and brought out more of the sensitive side of Robbie, the lonely boy alone in the crowd that surrounded him.

Just when that had settled the listener's ear, hi-hat drumming and the piano-riffing chords of 'Let Me Entertain You' battered the ears and shattered the just-minted picture of Robbie sat quietly humming. 'Let Me Entertain You' was the most brash of Robbie's recordings to date, a *tour de force* both musically and lyrically. Describing himself in the song as the burning effigy of what he used to be, Rob was no longer dependent upon four band-mates for a profile or a career: this was top pop music on his own terms.

As the album came to a close, 'Killing Me' was another burning, bitter assault on abuse, defencelessness, weakness and frustration. In the jaunty shuffle of 'Clean', Robbie was thinking hard about a new-found detox lifestyle, weaned off all the vision-blurring dross that a life lived through a lens incurs. But the song's ending – collapsing in upon itself in a psychedelic, swirling haze – suggested that the two minutes of cleanliness of the song might be an overstatement. Innocence, truth and honesty colour the lovely closing track, 'Baby Girl Window'. If the song itself was still looking for ways to take the pain away, then – after ten tracks of bitterness, aggravation, celebration, love and frustration – this was the track to do it, a lovely way to round off a scorching album.

What was very striking was how different the album was to most of Take That's material. It's not a new occurrence for a boy- or girl-band member to leave and proceed to say that they never really liked that type of music anyway. The problem is, this leaves their sizeable fan base feeling betrayed, like their hero/heroine was just going through the motions because it was a good earner. Robbie, however, was writing material that would by definition appeal to a much broader market than his former boy-band incarnation. Brian Harvey of East 17 says this is a common dilemma faced by the non-songwriters in pop bands: 'As much as the stuff by East 17 might not have been what I was into, I suppose some members of Take That probably weren't into their stuff either. However, Gary was writing and giving them their hits and putting them where they were. You just have to decide if it's right for you or not.'

Looking at the track-listing for *Life Thru a Lens* in hindsight, you would expect sales to be enormous. Yet, at first, they most certainly weren't. The choice of singles was poor and was reflected in average chart positions that eventually began to threaten Robbie's solo career being able to carry on at all. 'Old Before I Die' was a Britpop iden-tikit song with an odd video that Robbie later said left him 'chafed' from jumping off speakers – it was a No. 2 hit in April 1997, but sold almost 100,000 less than the pre-ceding George Michael cover. Furthermore, Robbie looked bloated and tired in the live performance video. 'Lazy Days' was more promising, a rich string-laden song, but one which saw sales plummet to 77,000 and peak at a relatively lowly No. 8 in the charts. Much worse was to come with the dreadful 'South of the Border', which was only ever going to sound like cod-Oasis – the public were unimpressed, with less than 45,000 sales barely scraping it into the Top Twenty at No. 18.

The parallels with Take That's own first three singles are striking – huge invest-ment and high expectations at the record company were simply not being met by results. The album proved to be no magic pill either at first. Unfortunately, sales were disappointing and initially the record seemed to have stalled below 40,000 copies sold. This was coming from a boy-band member whose previous group had sold over 10 million albums worldwide. In short, Robbie's solo career was in crisis.

Then, in the second week of December 1997, everything changed. Robbie Williams released 'Angels', the fourth single off the album. It's difficult to write much about 'Angels' that hasn't already been said, the career-defining track that relaunched Rob-bie's fading solo ambitions and has since made a laughing stock of a million TV audi-tionees, as well as being officially 'the most played first song at weddings'.

The track was already out there on his début album, but because the album sales were so low most punters were simply unaware of the track's existence. Astonishingly, it stalled in the charts at No. 4 (it would go on to be a festive chart re-entry). The song was the first that Robbie and Guy Chambers had written together and is regularly voted in the top five of countless 'Best Song Ever' polls. It's slushy but not too slushy, dramatic but not histrionic, a simple chord structure but one that pulls the heart strings in the way that the best songs always do, and almost ten years on from its release it is still a song that will get turned up when it appears on the radio. If Robbie Williams had never released another record in his life, he would have deserved the reputation he maintains today on the basis of 'Angels' alone.

The promo video was a clever piece of repackaging; shot in grainy black and white, it carried a feel of the work of Anton Corbijn, famous for still and celluloid work with Depeche Mode and, most famously, U2 during *The Joshua Tree* period. Robbie the booze-guzzling ex-boy-band star suddenly looked stylish, trim, cool and emotional. The track is almost hackneyed now because you have heard it so many times and seen the video clip endlessly too, but it is justifiably a watershed moment for Robbie. Aside from all the hyperbole about his lifestyle, habits, celeb girlfriends and the like, 'Angels', if you listen carefully, tells you what you actually need to know about Robbie Williams – that he is a gifted singer and brilliant performer. Just listen to a thousand average or worse singers missing the high notes and you will see what I mean.

'HE IS A GIFTED SINGER AND BRILLIANT PERFORMER.'

He has said that the track took no more than half an hour to write. Its impact must make that the most lucrative half-hour's work in music history. What 'Angels' did was catapult Robbie from former boy-band star to bona fide solo talent; it pushed sales of *Life Thru a Lens* from around the 100,000 mark to near a million (at the time of writing the album has passed the 2 million mark); it transformed his fan base from teenage girls to pretty much anyone over the age of about 5; it changed *everything*.

Life Thru a Lens eventually hit the top spot in the album charts a full seven months after it was first released and spent more than two years on the listings, providing Robbie with a platform from which one of the most astonishing, energizing and above all entertaining pop careers for decades was launched. Many artists have left boy bands with an eye to a winning solo career. Most of them have crashed desperately after a couple of well-promoted singles: they simply don't have the quality to support the audience their previous career enjoyed. Robbie's first solo album (eventually) staggered everyone – five hit singles, two of them among the greatest of the era, and one of them a hot contender (justifiably alongside such luminary tracks as Lennon's 'Imagine' and Queen's 'Bohemian Rhapsody') for the greatest hit single of all time (sales to date are just shy of 1 million, sadly falling short of the Top 100 singles of all-time sales). The starry-eyed boy from the Potteries had finally got there.

Robbie Williams Solo Artist had arrived.

CHALK AND CHEESE

Just how colossal the impact of 'Angels' was on Robbie's profile could be seen in the following months. For one, he was chosen to front the first ever pay-per-view concert on Sky television, *Robbie Williams Live at the Forum*, in 1998. A lengthy run of adverts plugged the show, which was introduced by 'anarchic' DJ-turned-presenter Chris Evans. The ads showed Robbie knocking on doors in the street – a throwback to his days selling double-glazing, perhaps? – offering to perform in their lounges. Most doors are slammed in his face until someone recognizes him and asks him in … which is exactly what Sky were offering you the chance for: Robbie in your living room.

Just as 'Back for Good' altered the industry and public's perception of Gary Barlow as a songsmith, so too did 'Angels' with Robbie – in June 1998 he won the prestigious Nordoff-Robbins Award for 'Best Newcomer'. After this, the gongs just piled in, including 'Best Male' at the MTV Awards (he was also nominated for 'Best Song' and 'Best Album'); 'Solo Artist of the Year' at the *GQ* Awards; and was eighty-fifth in middle-aged magazine *Mojo*'s Top 100 Artists of All Time. Brit Awards? At the time of writing he has fourteen, plus a special Brits 25 award for 'Best Single of the Past 25 Years' for 'Angels'.

There was a rash of Robbie Williams singles from late 1997 until August 2000 that, in retrospect, were a creative high point and which would make any other artist green with envy. 'Angels' was followed by 'Let Me Entertain You', complete with a KISS-like make-up and lycra video, supposedly causing great annoyance to Gene Simmons & Co., but not to Robbie when it hit No. 3 and shifted nearly a quarter of a million copies. Then came 'Millennium', with the hilarious James Bond spoof video which, for a while, made some think Robbie would actually make the best new Bond – it was a No. 1 song and doubled sales of the previous single. 'No Regrets', a more subtle turn, reached No. 4, and was co-written with Neil Tennant from the Pet Shop Boys and Neil

Hannon from The Divine Comedy, with a much darker video involving a sombre-looking Robbie and leaking fuel (Robbie later famously dedicated this to each of his former band mates at his career-defining Knebworth performance). 'Strong' was perhaps, ironically, the weakest of the bunch but still a solid effort at No. 4, while 'She's the One', formerly written and recorded by World Party supremo Karl Wallinger, who had worked with Chambers in the past when the latter had also been a member of that band, was another No. 1 song which guarantees Robbie a place in the karaoke Top Ten if not the No. 1 spot. Finally there came 'Rock DJ', with its macabre (and partly banned) video showing Robbie ripping off his actual flesh to impress the ladies. Nearly 600,000 people bought this and sent it to No. 1 too.

Robbie cleverly – and bravely – took on the festival circuit too, with an unlikely triumph at V98 in front of a field of largely indie kids smoking weed and getting pissed. Other pop bands have been booed off stage or worse – 50 Cent was famously showered with bottles at the rock-oriented Reading Festival – but Robbie seemed to rise to the challenge and in the process captured an entirely new section of fans. He was quickly becoming the artist that everyone wanted.

In 1998 Robbie travelled to Sri Lanka for UNICEF to highlight the work needed to immunize children against polio, an illness that kills and yet can be totally eradicated through vaccines. He accompanied Ian Dury, who had suffered from the disease himself since the age of 5. At the time Robbie was quoted as saying, 'What I worry about at home doesn't matter. I want to see how people smile in the face of adversity and carry on. I feel so much more serene and relaxed here.'

In the sad aftermath of the late Ian Dury's death, a tribute concert was organized at London's Brixton Academy. I was fortunate enough to be working backstage on the night. The dark, winding corridors of the beautiful Academy building were quite literally heaving with celebrities and musical icons, all drawn to the event by Dury's legend and massive reputation within the industry: Mick Jones of The Clash was there, Angelina Jolie was there, countless TV faces and so on.

At the end of one corridor there seemed to be a constant log-jam of people, usually a clear sign of some super-high-profile celeb in the building. It was, of course, Robbie Williams. In my opinion, he turned more heads that night than anyone else in the building.

The tabloids couldn't get enough of Robbie. For most of his career, he has been 'linked' (meaning 'seen with' but not always acknowledged as a couple) to various high-profile and beautiful females on an almost daily basis: Nicole Appleton, Geri Halliwell, Andrea from The Corrs, Denise Van Outen, Mel C (he seemed at one point to be going for the full spice rack), Anna Friel and Rod Stewart's ex, Rachel Hunter.

In 2005 Robbie sued British publishing groups MGN Limited, publisher of the *People*, and Northern & Shell PLC, publisher of *Star* and *Hot Stars* magazines, after stories they ran suggested that he'd had numerous homosexual encounters with strangers. They lost and agreed to publish prominent apologies and pay damages and legal costs.

It is a great contradiction of Robbie's career – probably deliberately – that although we know so much about him, in many ways we know nothing. For example, no one who is close to Robbie Williams calls him Robbie. It's Rob. 'Robbie' is a larger-than-life character that the British public know and seem to love. Sometimes he says things that make you cringe, sometimes he makes you laugh out loud and sometimes it is plain sadness he elicits. However, it is not Rob but Robbie doing that. As far back as his first solo album, he was suggesting as much: 'I'm still finding myself right now. I'd like to revert back to being seen as Robbie, the cheeky chappie who's a nice bloke to have around. Everything was cool when I was Robbie. It was like, "Hey, isn't everything brilliant! It's ace. Brilliant!" That's what I'd like to become again. I'd rather people get Robbie than Robert. Sure, I want to be myself with certain people who I'm really close with, but most people who meet me don't know Robert, they only know Robbie. And that's how I want to be seen, at least in public.'

Robbie compounded the progress made by 'Angels' with a swift release of his second album – modestly plugged on his own T-shirt at numerous festival appearances with the words 'The Second Album's Even Better'. By that stage it was no surprise when *I've Been Expecting You* became Robbie's second No. 1 solo album on its release in November 1998. The cover, showing his by now familiar sidelong smile, suggested a confidence and security at odds with the confrontational glare of *Life Thru a Lens*, but the opening track soon dispelled the myth. Clattering in like a classic Oasis B-side, 'Strong' carried a fantastic, witty and self-deprecating lyric but was an ordinary musical backdrop to open the new album. The CD booklet presented a Robbie high on the Hollywood lifestyle, with swimming pools and gorgeous women in attendance, but much of the content of the album seemed to present an unsure guy hiding an insecurity behind a razor-sharp cool image.

'No Regrets' was one such track, while 'Millennium' appeared a brash statement of style and cool, but even here Robbie's lyrics concerned our vulnerability at the hands of fate in a world of plastic surgery, falseness and solitude – hardly the stuff of dreams. Robbie rapped about the sarcasm in his eyes over a stylish sample from the theme to the 1967 Bond movie *You Only Live Twice*.

The other songs on the album were, without exception, strong tracks – full of heart and style, lyrically witty and self-examining. 'Phoenix from the Flames' had a

McCartney flavour to the melody which leapt from lush arrangement to brisk piano phrasing and fluent lead guitar. The lyrics again set Robbie and partner up against the world, filled with internal struggle and a need to build walls against a world outside. On 'Win Some Lose Some' Robbie was more resigned to the vagaries of fate, as another relationship fell apart to the backing vocals of one-time All Saint Nicole Appleton. The Latin cool of 'Grace' masks more immolation, showing a singer desperate to get a relationship to work against the odds. 'Jesus in a Camper Van' – apart from having one of the best titles of any album track that year, and a cool shuffle to carry the song along – took to pieces the notion of being an icon or a messiah for anyone, the character of the song so battered by the experience that he sleeps with the light on and admits he's done all he could (notably, Robbie and Guy co-wrote the song with Canadian songwriter Loudon Wainwright III).

'Heaven from Here' is a gentle, lilting guitar, bass and drum song with a gorgeous melody but more modest lyrics. There's more self-belief in 'Heaven from Here' than any song so far – here's a relationship that's working because the voice of the song seems more able to put into the relationship than declaring a need to take from it. However, then the sinister descending verse and glorious, string-driven chorus of 'Karma Killer' took Robbie's listeners back into a world of recrimination and accusation, but there's a resilience in there too: however much has been taken, there's enough left to stay strong. And if all else fails, there were those screaming, barking dogs at the close of the song to keep the harm at bay. Listening for the first time, Robbie's fans found *I've Been Expecting You* up to this point as good as expected. But, just when you thought it was safe to go back in the water, up came the killer track.

'THE WORLD FELT IT KNEW JUST A LITTLE MORE ABOUT THE DARK SIDE OF THE UK'S HOTTEST SOLO PERFORMER.'

Like 'Angels', 'She's the One' has become one of the most-loved songs of the era, another chart-topping single with a drop-dead-gorgeous melody, drum-tight arrangement, and Robbie in vulnerable mode. Robbie's voice is light and soulful at once, a real performance rather than simply a singing of the lyric, and – like 'Angels' – it remains a career highlight.

There was a distinctly Sixties flavour to 'Man Machine', a Monkees-like opening to a track that nevertheless rocks out into Oasis territory by the time the chorus comes around. There was no lightweight material on the album at all, and by the time the

closing track, 'These Dreams', rounded the collection off, the world felt it knew just a little more about the dark side of the UK's hottest solo performer.

It was a foregone conclusion that the album would hit the top spot, and it did so on its release in early November 1998. By then, Robbie Williams was the biggest solo star in Britain.

In stark contrast, Gary Barlow's solo career had been floundering for some time. Previously I have said that 'Angels' dealt a killer blow to Gary's aspirations. That's not entirely accurate: to qualify that, it stopped for various reasons, but Robbie Williams's career-saving single was without doubt a major factor in the disheartening turnaround in Gary's fortunes. In fact, Gary had already had worrying chart positions for the No. 11 hit 'So Help Me Girl' in July 1997 (sales had more than halved from the previous single at 75,000), but with the release of 'Angels' that Christmas all media attention flipped to Robbie as the new great white hope. Post-'Angels', Gary did not hit the Top Ten again.

It was a harsh and unforgiving backlash, no doubt about that, and not one that Gary had incited. In interviews he was always polite: he was (and still is) widely regarded as a humble man – driven, yes, but with his feet on the ground. In Robbie Williams the press seemed to have found themselves a *bête noire* and that, naturally, was infinitely more appealing than a family man with more interest in soda than coke. Drugs, sex and rock and roll sell papers, simple as that. So once Robbie started delivering songs like 'Angels' and 'Let Me Entertain You', as well as living the high life of a global celebrity, the writing was effectively on the wall for Gary's solo career.

Gary Barlow

At times Robbie was the most prolific verbal graffiti artist, spraying out scores of biting one-liners and brutal put-downs Gary's way. Without doubt the biggest friction from Take That's split seemed to be between Gary and Robbie (closely followed and then surpassed by the bad blood between Robbie and Nigel Martin-Smith). Early on in their respective solo careers, newspaper headlines such as 'Gary's Richer than Robbie' and 'Take Sides and Pick a Winner' fuelled the tension that already existed. Gary later said that the public love nothing more than a duel, and for a while they certainly got that with these two former band-mates. To be fair to Robbie, in his first interview since leaving the band he actually said in *The Face*, 'I am never ever going to slag them off. Never. Take That did a lot for me, moulded a huge part of my life and the whole base of where I am going to go from here.' He even denied there were any rows when he was in the band.

Nonetheless, the stereotyping of Gary as some kind of dour Northerner with a firm grasp on his wallet was relentless and in direct contrast to LA-living, famous-bird-shagging, vice-battling, multi-million-selling Robbie Williams, and it was easy to see who the tabloids would prefer.

Even something as superficial as their looks worked against Gary. He'd never made a secret of the fact that he struggled with style, whereas Robbie seemed to be able to wear anything and look cool. Gary was that very odd mix between – on a bad day – the better-looking brother of Tyrone from Coronation Street and – on a good day – shades of Tom Cruise. Robbie just always looked … well, like Robbie.

Despite earlier protestations to the contrary, Robbie appeared happy to fuel this duel. While Gary remained relatively tight-lipped about Robbie, Robbie made many quips about his former colleague. In December 1997 Gary and Robbie performed (separately) at Princess Diana's Concert of Hope, which saw both join the end-of-set climax for a group rendition of The Beatles' 'Let It Be'. The papers talked of a reconciliation, but there was to be nothing of that sort yet.

Even when Robbie was standing at the podium picking up another Brit Award, he couldn't resist another dig: 'I was always the talented member of the band.' Famously, the cruel *Rock Profiles* spoof of Howard and Gary by *Little Britain*'s David Walliams and Matt Lucas showed up the polar opposites of fortunes being enjoyed by the former band-mates, not least when these two comedians were invited to present an award to Robbie himself.

Howard Donald

Ben Ofoedu has one theory about why Robbie stole the march on Gary: 'The big issue was that Robbie was the underdog. It's that British mentality: Eddie the Eagle, the favourite should never win. Gary was not the underdog, Robbie was the cheeky-chappy underdog, and that played a big factor in how people perceived those two artists, I think. Plus he is an amazing talent, without a shadow of a doubt. His songs came through and blew everyone away.'

'THE LIFE OF A SINGER-SONGWRITER IS TERRIBLY LONELY.'

Nick Raymonde explained to me how challenging the solo years were for Gary. 'He had to be given his head because this was his opportunity and he'd earned his right, in my view, to make whatever record he wanted to. Gary's record was maybe put out too quickly for Take That fans to make the leap in styles, but I actually think it was a pretty good record. It sold a lot of copies too, regardless of what people think, but the expectations on him were enormous. Several hundred thousand sales is the stuff of dreams for many acts, but for someone like Gary, especially at that point in his career, it's not enough. You would have wanted that record to sell a million copies.

'I think it was hard for Gary. There was enormous amount of pressure on him to deliver a record when he probably just wanted to have a minute and take his time – the reality was he needed to make a record that was going to sell a million copies. Also, suddenly you've not got your mates around you. I've worked with both solo artists and bands, and I think the life of a singer-songwriter is terribly lonely. If you've got a band of lads around you, it makes the whole thing much more manageable. But if you're out there on your own touring with musicians that are hired guns, it's not a real family. When you're in a band, it's that gang thing. Meanwhile, Robbie was self-destructing and everyone was going "poor lad" and somehow certain people seemed to be blaming Gary for it. It had nothing to do with him.'

Once the tide had turned, it seemed there was nothing Gary could do to fight it. His excellent album title-track briefly restored the balance of power, hitting No. 7, but the slide had begun. Only two more solo singles were released: 'Stronger' hit No. 16, but by then Robbie had unleashed 'Angels', 'Let Me Entertain You', 'No Regrets' and 'Strong' on a doting nation. That's hard company to compete with by anybody's standards. Finally, 'For All That You Want', released in October 1999, slipped up badly at No. 24, by which times sales had dipped to less than 20,000. A month later Robbie's 'She's the One' sold forty times more copies.

By now there were conflicting stories in the papers: some suggesting Gary's record label were thinking of dropping him if the next single – 'Lie to Me' – didn't do well; others denying this and saying he was still a priority artist. 'Gary is a very important artist on the BMG roster and we look forward to a long and fruitful relationship with him.' The next album, originally titled *Stronger* but then altered to *Twelve Months, Eleven Days*, only charted at No. 35 with sales of 18,000, a shocking 264,000 less than his début album. Meanwhile, Robbie was about to sell his five millionth album.

Gary's last single remained unreleased and he was quickly to be found writing in studios with other performers.

By April 2003 Robbie Williams had signed a record contract with EMI for a reported figure of £80 million. Meanwhile, despite his substantial wealth and success behind the scenes as a songwriter, Gary Barlow's official website was closed down. The exact date that the site was 'de-tagged' was 17 March, which effectively erased it from the internet. There were stories of Gary staying for long periods in his mansion and over-eating; he later revealed that at his lowest he would hate using his credit card over the phone, 'because when I said [my name was] Gary Barlow, people would just laugh or sneer. Not a good experience at all.' The comparisons were stark.

With Gary, there was an inevitability once he had retired to the shadows that Robbie would grab all the headlines. Yet closer inspection of Gary's career in the immediate post-solo years before Take That re-formed reveals he was hardly dormant and, to be frank, earned an absolute fortune. Among the massive hits he wrote were songs for Delta Goodrem ('Lost Without You'), large chunks of Charlotte Church's catalogue, as well as writing and producing music with Elton John, Donny Osmond, Gloria Estefan and Christina Aguilera. Some perspective is needed on Gary Barlow's 'failed career'. While Robbie was undoubtedly the immediate and meteoric solo success story post-Take That in terms of profile, fame and to some degree songs, Gary did not exactly sit on his laurels. Early visions of him singing in a pie-and-mash club, doing 'Gary Barlow presents the songs of Take That', are merely the stuff of now outdated stand-up comedy routines. Even when the world was fêting Robbie, Gary remained an incredibly wealthy man whose songwriting prowess was sought after universally by major labels around the world. Plus, he certainly still enjoyed a celebrity lifestyle – when Elton John got married to long-term partner David Furnish in late 2005, Gary Barlow was invited to sing at the hen party.

Many commentators and observers (myself included) hold the opinion that Gary Barlow was treated shockingly over his solo career, regardless of how the stellar re-formation of Take That in 2005 has altered the public's perception of him once again. Back in the mid-Nineties the pressure that was piled on him to be 'the new George Michael' was oppressive, and he was, after all, still only 25 when he released 'Forever Love'. The pressure on him musically was only exceeded by comments about his weight, his looks, his supposedly 'boring' lifestyle and other peripheral factors. Then along comes Robbie, with his birds, booze and banging on about his former bandmate, yet seeming to have a Midas touch that was in exact inverse proportion to Gary's profile. Whenever Gary was portrayed in the media during those difficult years, it was hard not to wonder how he must have felt. When he cancelled one set of shows, it was never mentioned that he donated the interest generated on ticket revenues in the meantime to a children's charity. When he chatted politely to Michael Parkinson one time, you could almost sense the frustration, the anger. Even taking only his modest solo career itself and ignoring the glorious new material that Take That have released since their re-formation, Gary Barlow is without doubt one of Britain's most sublime pop writers of recent times and as such should be applauded roundly. With or without Take That, and certainly with or without Robbie Williams.

Besides, Gary's most important creation came in August 2000 when he and wife Dawn – a former dancer with Take That – celebrated their first-born child, Daniel. He was followed two years later by a younger sister, Emily.

PEOPLE IN
GLASS HOUSES

ALL THE RHETORIC THE POP world can muster as to why Robbie Williams made such an impact as a solo artist and yet Gary Barlow didn't is crucially missing one other major point – why isn't Mark Owen also a huge solo star? It was Mark whom most girls fancied, it was Mark who got more magazine front covers than anyone else, more fan mail, more wedding proposals, more presents; it was Mark that all the mums preferred. And yet, once the band was over, he couldn't get his solo career off the ground, and it was patently not for want of personal and financial investment and sheer bloody hard work.

Mark was third out of the blocks with his first solo single, only four months after Gary's début single, and three months after Robbie's 'Freedom'. He easily soared to No. 3 with 'Child', but by all accounts it was clearly a dreadful song. It sounded heavily inspired by Lennon but fell way short of such lofty standards. The music business was going to chew him up if he continued to release songs like that. Interestingly, though, despite harsh critical reviews the track actually sold very heavily, almost 200,000 copies passing through the tills.

Michael Metcalf of GMTV has worked with Mark many times and says that his professionalism is hard to ignore: 'We did our summer road show one time and he came out to Spain and we went out for dinner the night before till late. Yet he turned up the next morning bang on time and ready to go.'

Fortunately, his next release was the uplifting pop song 'Clementine', which seemed to briefly offer a strong future for Mark's solo ideas and charted high, again at No. 3. Worryingly, sales were almost half that of 'Child' and there were signs that the public and media were struggling to enthuse about his solo material. Sadly, by the time of his third single, 'I Am What I Am', public interest had largely dissipated and the song just sneaked into the Top Thirty, shifting only 26,500 copies in total.

Mark's début album was called *Green Man* and was a sound effort, but it similarly failed to ignite the public's enthusiasm enough to lift it past No. 33 in the album charts. Mark had certainly got the right pieces of the jigsaw in place – the record was produced by the legendary John Leckie, and it proved to be a steady seller, eventually making gold status in the UK, registering sales in excess of 100,000 copies. With Take That's following being so international, tours across several continents were a given for Mark however the UK reacted to his solo work. Thus in 1997 and 1998 he played shows all across Europe and the Far East.

Nonetheless, his solo profile remained modest, so Take That fans were delighted to hear the news that Mark was going to be a contestant on the 2002 series of *Celebrity Big Brother*, the ten-day Channel 4 charity reality show. Along with him for the ride in the Big Brother house were fellow contestants such as comedian and presenter Les Dennis, glamour model Melinda Messenger, former daytime TV presenter Anne Diamond, comedienne Sue Perkins and musician Goldie.

Mark was quickly installed as the bookies' favourite, and their faith in his popularity proved correct when he polled a vast majority of the votes to crown him the winner, ahead of the other two finalists, Dennis (christened 'Les Miserables' by one tabloid for his depressed demeanour, he was Mark's preferred champion) and Messenger. As runner-up, while Les Dennis was evicted and interviewed by Davina, Mark was left alone in the house to contemplate his win and, literally as Les was speaking, Mark broke down in tears. 'He's got a fantastic aura, a really brilliant aura – look at him. That's so sweet,' said Dennis, obviously touched.

It was actually very moving to see Mark moved to tears by the warm reception he received when he emerged as the winner. He seemed genuinely taken aback by the public's support. Given it was only six years since he was probably doing fifteen or twenty interviews a day, he was oddly stunned and clearly under-confident in front of the show's presenter Davina McCall. 'I'm a bit out of practice, sorry,' he readily admitted. He spoke very highly of Les Dennis, saying, 'He's been through a lot, he was a star and he helped me get through it,' and generally came across as a very humble, likeable and grounded chap. There was no sense of inflated ego either, with Mark joking, 'I had a moment where I woke up and at one end of the room Les Dennis was shaving, and at the other end Goldie was putting on his aftershave. I thought, *What am I doing here?*'

Unlike the 2005 series of the show, none of the contestants were paid to take part. Instead the phone votes raised hundreds of thousands of pounds for the Centrepoint homeless charity, the National Missing Persons Helpline, the Rethink mental illness charity and the Samaritans.

With this amazing high-profile launch pad, Mark put out his new single, which also happened to be his finest song to date, 'Four Minute Warning'. The pretext of the lyrics were essentially what you would do if the nuclear conflict left you with 240 seconds to live, and this led to some very entertaining interviews with the former That-er! Happily, the song fared well and charted at No. 4, staying in the charts for two months and selling a respectable 82,000 copies. Oddly, the momentum of this resurgence seemed to be lost almost straight away, and following 'Alone Without You' (which reached No. 26) his second record company in a row dropped him from their books, despite a decent second album with November 2003's *In Your Own Time*. The simple problem was that not enough people bought the record and it floundered at No. 59 in the UK album charts with poor sales, almost 100,000 less than his début effort.

'NO ONE CAN DENY HIS STAGE PRESENCE.'

This left Mark without a record deal and thus he immediately started his own label, Sedna Records. This is a situation that many former pop idols find themselves in – the Spice Girls' Mel C had taken a similar path in 2004. These stars have the funds and feel frustrated by the myopia of the business, eventually deciding that controlling their own music is the best way forward. The problem can be that many cynics see this as little more than vanity recording (a harsh standpoint and one that I personally don't agree with).

Besides, Mark was still attracting some big-name contributors, including, during a spell in early 2004, recording in LA, the likes of former REM drummer Joey Waronker, ex-Jellyfish founder Roger Manning Jr, Greg Kurstin and Dan Rothschild. The third album, *How the Mighty Fall*, was produced by none other than Tony Hoffer, famous for his work with Beck, Supergrass, Turin Brakes and The Thrills. For Mark, who once had a lizard called Nirvana, these collaborators were the stuff of his dreams.

Sales were still low, with June 2004's 'Makin' Out' only reaching No. 30. The album fared even worse, hitting the chart position of 295. However, with a sizeable publishing deal signed to former Take That label BMG, and an album track 'In the Boogie' being added to the European soundtrack of the hit Brad Pitt and Angelina Jolie movie *Mr & Mrs Smith* by the close of 2005, the omens were finally good for Mark's solo material. Even when news broke of Take That's reunion tour in late 2005, Mark was still determined to launch his solo career: 'I set up my own recording studio at my home in the Lake District and have paid out for all my own CDs to be produced. I don't care how well my albums do – it's my hobby and I do it all for my own fun. I don't think I'll ever stop producing them because I love writing.'

Even if observers are doubtful about Mark's solo recorded output, no one can deny his stage presence. Top music writer Ben Myers went to one of Mark Owen's solo gigs at the famous punk venue The 100 Club back in the summer of 1997: 'Though there was a certain air of tragedy to seeing Mark Owen resorting to playing a dingy basement dive – albeit one with a rich and significant musical heritage – to a crowd of several hundred or so curious fans and passers by, it was also, quite unexpectedly, a joyous occasion. Mark had the moves, charisma and the ability to project that comes from playing arenas. He even did a rousing rendition of Prince's "Let's Go Crazy". I, for one, thought that out of all the ex-band members it was Mark who was going to succeed where the highly touted Gary and Robbie would fail, if only for his boundless energy and natural charm. How wrong I was …'

In typically understated fashion, Mark was happy to say that promoting his own records had sapped his Take That fortune: 'I earned a few million pounds from Take That, but instead of me splashing out on Ferraris and Porsches, the money has paid for my solo singles and albums.' Although, seeing the size and beauty of his North West home with a Range Rover in the drive, reports of Mark's wealth being 'blown' were hugely exaggerated at this time. One report around 2004 even alleged that Mark was looking for a day job, but he simply said, 'Doing it properly isn't cheap. These are my indulgences. I don't have a Ferrari, I have two albums.'

Korda Marshall, who'd signed Take That to RCA back in 1991, has a lot of time for Mark Owen, even though he wasn't moved enough to sign his solo career: 'It is not a music biz myth, it is true he's lovely. He's got a good voice – I don't think he's as talented as Robbie and I don't think he's as great a songwriter, if I am honest. I think the trouble with Mark's [solo] career was that he tried to make an indie rock album when his audience wasn't indie rock. He came and brought me the album and I remember he'd spent a lot of his money from Take That making this solo record. It wasn't for me, but you have to say he had the strength of his own convictions, he wanted to do it and he did it. Fair play to him for that.'

Shane Lynch from Boyzone understands how difficult it is for a former boy-band member to 'go solo' but finds this fact a little bemusing: 'All of a sudden you run into problems and in the context of being in a huge boy band before, that's a mind-blowing thing. You think, *How on earth have I got a problem? Where did this problem come from?* When somebody breaks up from a band and wants to go solo, if the radio stations don't play their record … well, forget it, mate, you ain't gonna have a hit. There's such a massive fan base already established, but it is so hard.'

Looking back at Mark's solo years, he has two very strong singles to his credit – 'Clementine' and 'Four Minute Warning' – yet for some reason the British public never backed him. They backed him in Take That, they backed him in the Big Brother house with several million phone votes, and they would back him again when Take That reformed, but they didn't back his solo records.

The post-Take That careers of Howard and Jason were even more low profile than those of Gary and Mark, but no less eventful. Jason had once said he might consider band management, but not a pop act, rather 'anything alternative and miserable – people who don't smile too much'. However, this career never transpired. Jason was the only member of Take That who did not pursue a solo career. He made no secret that he was very shy and found singing in front of people very hard – ironic given that the band's last arena tour was in front of hundreds of thousands of people.

For a whole year after the band finally parted ways, Jason relaxed in his house and recuperated from the frenzied five years he'd just experienced. He enjoyed a spell of acting, including an appearance on Channel 4's Lynda La Plante drama *Killernet*, playing a drug dealer called Brent Moyer. He even went on GMTV to promote North London play, *Gob*, which he was starring in (albeit only for a two-night run at the King's Head Theatre). 'He came in one morning for the show and was absolutely charming as usual,' recalls Michael Metcalf. Jason also undertook college courses studying sociology and psychology, went backpacking and travelled the world and generally caught his breath after five years of Take That insanity. Then, with his energy levels and morale restored, he started looking into more acting roles and was soon snapped up for a number of further theatre and TV roles. Most famously, he had a starring role in Sky One's *Dream Team* football soap.

For most of Take That's career Howard still lived with his parents. In the band's 1995 annual – by which time the group were already the biggest pop act on the planet – he said, 'I'm not in a hurry to move. I love my room. I've got me sink! I've got a kettle up there for whenever I want to make a brew. My keyboards are up there.' Howard had installed a home studio as far back as 1994 and was open about having demoed his own material, although it was never suggested this would lead to him leaving the band. After the split he started laying down tracks and eventually whispers started surfacing that he had written a solo album. Given that he sang on the actual Take That records, as well as live, and even wrote 'If This is Love' with David James on the band's second album, there was no reason to suspect he couldn't make a solo career work.

Unfortunately, Howard suffered even more of a struggle than Gary or Mark. After securing a small record deal and even filming a video for the scheduled August 1997 track 'Speak Without Words', the single and album were never released and Howard's solo hopes sank without trace. He'd even written a track for the then-rising star Kavana, but solo performing was not to be where he made his mark post-Take That.

On the 2005 ITV1 documentary Howard said, 'It was difficult to adjust after Take That split. It took a year for me to realize how difficult it was to carry on without them. I had to get used to the fact that I was no longer with the four friends I'd been with twenty-four hours a day for years.'

'IT TOOK A YEAR FOR ME TO REALIZE HOW DIFFICULT IT WAS TO CARRY ON WITHOUT THEM.'

Brian Harvey of East 17 totally related to this apparent emotional void that springs up when a big boy band disbands: 'Boy bands often happen overnight and it is all well and good while it is going well, but there is no training in the world to prepare you for the day that it starts going downhill. You're thrown in at the deep end because you were made a success overnight, usually very young, and you really get used to that, then suddenly it all stops. There was nothing to get me ready for the downfall and the bankruptcies and losing your money. You're just left on your own.

'When you are famous, everyone knows who you are, everyone knows your business, your private life, who you've been out with, what you've done wrong, and then all of a sudden you're just out there in the public on your own. You can't switch the fame off, it's too late, it's already happened. When you are starting up and you get the record deal, you start meeting famous people, you think your life is going to be like that forever, but it ain't.

'Another problem I can see they have endured is that you've just had your growing-up years in the public eye and suddenly no one wants to help you or give you a chance any more. You're just vulnerable when it all ends, you've got no protection, there is no management, there is no security picking you up, there is no one keeping other people away from you, you're just out in the open, and then it comes down to what sort of a person are you really: are you really as strong as you think you are? The downside can be just terrible, it cancels out a lot of the good.'

A bigger and actually far more important change was about to come to Howard's life when he had a daughter by the name of Grace. On the ITV1 documentary the two were filmed playing on a beach and the intimacy and love was very poignant. For many, the most telling comment of the entire documentary was when Howard explained why he had bought a house in Bournemouth: 'Because where my daughter goes, I go.' In an age where children are often mere celebrity accessories, this was a striking and refreshing statement.

Robbie continued to bait and snipe at some of his former band-mates occasionally, despite having established himself as the premier solo artist in the UK. Even as late as the spring of 2004 he was quoted as saying, 'The rest couldn't sing or dance and had to be in bed by 9 p.m.' Presumably he was just poking fun, but it seemed churlish when he was doing so well.

The media were always keen to highlight any tensions between him and his former colleagues. In 2003 a feature appeared in the *Daily Record* headlined 'Why I Hate Robbie by Take That's Howard Donald'. The printed text had no mention of the words 'why I hate Robbie', however, and merely served to show just how amiable and mellow Howard seems to be. Although it says he can't stand listening to Robbie's music, this was because 'It's not the sort of stuff I would buy, but millions seem to like it.'

He went on, 'Robbie has established himself and is a great performer, I suppose. He is a megastar now but without Take That he would be nothing. The band was his apprenticeship. His criticisms of me don't bother me. Robbie is Robbie and all he has done since he left the group is take the piss.'

Yet Howard was about to embark on an entirely new career, which would see him jetting across Europe once more, as a sought-after funky house DJ. Boy George had already made this transition, and famous nightclub owner and *Celebrity Love Island* winner Fran Cosgrave also plays his DJ sets to thousands of people every night, but Howard was the most high-profile former boy-band member to take on this guise. 'Thankfully, I had enough money to go on a long holiday and think about what I really wanted to do. I don't even listen to pop music any more.' What he wanted to do was simple: DJ.

Howard had done some DJ work before Take That took off, not least because he was either working in clubs or going clubbing with his friends in his days as a dancer. He didn't use decks during his first spell in Take That – there was no spare time for a start – but once the dust had settled from the initial split he found himself being drawn to playing tunes again. Within a few months he was a DJ people wanted to book. 'I'm in the lucky position where people come to see me because I'm a name, then come back because of the music.' Interestingly, once his DJ career had taken off, Howard seemed to have an altogether different view on releasing his own music: 'I wouldn't do a solo career now. There are too many good singers and solo artists out there. The music business is a difficult place to be in these days … I want to be a successful DJ and not to live off the name of Take That. But I'm definitely proud of my past. It's not like I'm embarrassed by it.' Finally, he said, 'When I became a dad it mellowed me out but it didn't stop me wanting to work.'

PLAY TO WIN

Don Henley once said, 'If you're gonna write songs, you've gotta have a life.' Well, Robbie Williams had certainly experienced a life like no other up until the turn of the new millennium and, if trials and tribulations were grist for his mill, then he has enough material to last him a lifetime. However – and this is entirely a matter of subjective, personal opinion – I think that since 'Rock DJ' Robbie hasn't quite lived up to his own fabulously high standards. Sales figures prove me wrong, of course, with no single solo artist being able to touch the vast numbers of records, tickets and T-shirts he sells. Yet at the time of writing there is that feeling that Robbie is in a period of, if not fallow, then certainly lower-key releases.

September 2000 saw the release of Robbie's third solo album, *Sing When You're Winning*, another No. 1 hit record. By now he was well established as Britain's leading solo male pop performer, and perhaps the biggest name in UK music, period. Modestly recognizing this accomplishment, the CD sleeve saw a team of footballing Robbies at play in a cup final – celebrating victory, protecting their groins from a curling free kick, elbowing opponents out of the way – right up to the celebratory post-match bath, with Rob's 'tackle' carefully obscured by another Robbie's arm. The message was clear: 'Robbie was a winning team.' Just in case anyone misinterpreted Williams's ego at large, he also represented himself as a bunch of supporters pissing up a wall *en route* to the match, and as a dodgy spiv offering shady tickets outside the ground. 'Take me seriously, but for Christ's sake don't take me seriously.' It was a smart profile.

The new collection was again produced and co-written by Guy Chambers ('as much Robbie as I am', as the dedication has it) and on a few tracks a handful of co-writers. The album provided Robbie with another four Top Ten hits, including among them another No. 1. 'Let Love Be Your Energy', the opening track, just made the Top Ten in March 2001, a heavyweight single with a crunching chorus and Sixties flavour to the chord structures. 'Better Man' was slower, soulful and acoustic, a lyric confirming a growing maturity in Robbie's life, or maybe just a growing maturity in his song-writing. Chambers's arrangement was lush, Robbie's vocal warm and honest.

The album's natural chart-topper was the aforementioned 'Rock DJ'. Spicing up a heavy dose of Ian Dury influence in the opening bars with a bit of Barry White thrown in for good measure, Robbie's very English rap, the spinning string arrangement and pumping bass lines made for an irresistible, catchy track that lit up the clubs and discos of summer 2000. 'Supreme' was another huge hit at the end of the year, reaching No. 4 with its articulate referencing of the feminist anthem 'I Will Survive'.

'Kids' matched the perfect pop poise of Princess Kylie with a naughty-boy-made-good version of Robbie (for every new song there seemed to be a new Robbie available). The rhyme sequence of 'economy', 'sodomy', 'monogamy', 'Billy Connolly' and 'ornithology' is fantastic, Robbie's Staffordshire accent rapping out the lines laconically. It hit the No. 2 slot effortlessly.

The slow groove of 'If It's Hurting You' followed 'Kids', a country-tinted ballad of shared pain and heartache that sat the listener down again after a dance around the bedroom. 'Singing for the Lonely' was upbeat but lilting, the Oasis-friendly rock of the previous album less in evidence as this collection progressed. Yet if Robbie's lyrics are to be interpreted as autobiographical at all, then it was clear that his self-dissecting was not going to be hidden under an acoustic guitar and jaunty bass line. 'Singing for the Lonely' is a painful piece of self-examination, neatly rounded off with a bit of reggae bass and gentle backing vocals. You can wrap the gift up, but you can still feel what's inside.

Similarly, the slow acoustic shuffle of 'Love Calling Earth' is about hurt and fear, inadequacy encompassed in such a rich and warming track that The Carpenters could have written it. The wonderfully titled 'Knutsford City Limits' references not only the obvious Ike and Tina Turner song, but the rather posh Cheshire town north of Stoke known to most car drivers in the UK for the motorway service station that bears its name. From Knutsford to Texas in one easy move, 'Forever Texas' offered maybe another insight into Robbie's sense of self-worth, and in 'By All Means Necessary' he dissects the lifestyle of a starlet lost in a maze of celebrity shagging and selling herself for fifteen minutes' worth of fame. The album wrapped up with the divine 'Road to Mandalay', with its images of despair and sadness, loss and desolation.

It's a dangerous assumption that all the lyrics we read from a writer genuinely reflect his or her own sentiments and feelings. There is fiction, after all. But if Robbie was genuinely opening his heart in these songs it was a dark and troubled heart at the core. He might have played the clown, the Norman Wisdom of Nineties pop, but the legend of the tragic clown seemed appropriate if anybody took the trouble to read the lines. You didn't even have to read between them – the evidence was laid out before you.

Robbie's career was far from on the rocks: *Sing When You're Winning* sold over 2 million copies, almost as many as its predecessor (incredibly, *I've Been Expecting You* has passed the 2.6 million mark). Furthermore, his next step was to swerve wildly into a different genre altogether: crooning – a plausible but substantial risk even for someone with Robbie's voice.

You almost felt Robbie was delving into matters Sinatra for his own sense of adventure. As the most established singer in UK pop, Robbie Williams needed no speed-dating rush of new material to update a flagging career. Having reached the pinnacle of chart success and virtually unanimous critical acclaim, with three superb solo albums and fifteen big hit singles, Robbie could have taken time out and searched the wind for another 'Angels' or 'She's the One'. Instead, to his credit, he took a big risk … and pulled it off.

'TO HIS CREDIT, HE TOOK A BIG RISK … AND PULLED IT OFF.'

His fourth album, *Swing When You're Winning*, was a collection of standards from the era of Robbie's parents and earlier, Rat Pack songs and crooning ballads from the Fifties. An eighteen-piece orchestra was assembled at Sinatra's favoured spot, the Capitol Studios in Los Angeles. Although you might think this was a clever marketer's way of repackaging the star, Robbie had actually voiced interest in this genre many years previously, when Take That were in their heyday. 'I remember him running into my hotel room in Germany one night after a gig,' recalls Nick Raymonde. 'He burst in and said, totally out of the blue, "I want to make a record like Mack the Knife," and then he sang that song brilliantly, just standing there in the middle of the room. I just thought, *Jesus, this boy can sing*.'

From the outset it was clear that there was no irony involved here – full respect was shown to the original recordings of fantastic tunes such as 'Mack the Knife', 'Beyond the Sea' and 'Have You Met Miss Jones?', which featured heavily in the hit movie *Bridget Jones's Diary* and its accompanying soundtrack. The big hit, of course, was Robbie's duet with the divine Nicole Kidman on 'Something Stupid' – originally a hit for Frank and Nancy Sinatra – complete with super-kitsch video.

Robbie returned to the risky business of blending his and Frank's voices on a remake of 'It Was a Very Good Year'. Even Frank purists were impressed by the exercise, which could have gone so horribly wrong. 'One for My Baby', 'Mr Bojangles', 'They Can't Take That Away from Me' – all heart-wrenching classic ballads – were knocked out with a purity and clarity that proved Robbie's status as Mr All-Rounder, ironically the trait that probably best described the original artists who had covered these songs fifty or so years earlier.

'I JUST THOUGHT, JESUS, THIS BOY CAN SING.'

But in a sense, although it was a risk, and one successfully negotiated (the album was critically well received and was another No. 1 for Robbie, his second-best seller to date), the album represented a backward step for Robbie creatively. Perhaps the soul-baring of his writing so far had been a step too far emotionally, and perhaps a break from touching up the heart on his sleeve every six months was desperately needed, but *Swing When You're Winning* marked a two-year gap in Robbie's creative album output. The crest of the wave had been successfully ridden, but despite the No. 1 hit with Kidman, all the elements of Robbie's solo career to date that had been so appealing – the witty but incisive lyrics, the musical diversity born of his writing relationship with Guy Chambers, the blend of North Country rap, trippy dance tracks and grungy rock – had disappeared. It was as though, riding the fastest roller-coaster, Robbie stepped off to take some photos from the top. The pictures he took might have been great, but the roller-coaster wasn't running.

Much has been made of Robbie's apparent 'failure' to crack America. His first two albums were amalgamated and issued as *The Ego Has Landed*, but in a country famous for not understanding British humour the odds were always stacked against this Staffordshire Master of Joke Ceremonies. Any sarcasm, self-deprecation or witticisms Robbie came out with on the endless publicity he did were usually lost on the interviewers. Robbie worked very hard and, given his £80 million record deal, was encouraged all the way by his label, who were looking to the world's biggest record market to recoup some of their massive outlay. However, at the time of writing, despite Robbie living in a multi-million-pound home in Los Angeles (which, until his return to the UK in 2009, he had used as his main residence for five years), he remains, relative to the UK, only partially well known in the US.

With two more mega-selling albums to his name – *Escapology* and *Intensive Care* – plus a near 2 million-selling *Greatest Hits* compilation and a live album too, Robbie

Williams in the year 2005 stood as one of those rare artists who had sold more than 10 million albums in the UK alone. So I am sure he will not be reading my opinion that his more recent material is not as unique as his earlier solo work with anything other than contempt, not least as he will be doing so in one of his several multi-million-pound homes, with countless fans around the world who'll disagree with me. And to be fair, there is no one to match him at present in the UK. No one.

Korda Marshall of Warner Brothers Records, formerly of RCA, has a lot of time for Robbie. Speaking to the author for the first edition of this book in 2006, Korda said: 'He's come through brilliantly. Even now, when he is doing so well, I look back and remember the difficult times, when I was in hotel bars with Oasis and Robbie and all kind of things were going on; when he went on *TFI Friday* with Chris Evans and basically said, "I'm broke, I've got no money." Bless him, his strength of character, his strength of conviction and his talent have seen him swim into clear waters and make it work.

'I can't really think of many artists who can compare to what Robbie has done, not in the pop world. They will all try to copy Robbie but he has succeeded so much because he's ingenious at what he does. The other thing about Robbie is that he's got fantastic management. The whole IE management firm and the people behind Robbie have been brilliant at developing "Robbie", giving him space and time to evolve. The combination of his talent and their expertise and experience is mightily potent.'

'THEY WILL ALL TRY TO COPY ROBBIE.'

Boyzone's Shane Lynch is a big admirer of Robbie but hopes that his current sobriety and healthy mind remain – because Shane knows how demanding and exhausting the life of a pop star can be. 'I pray for Robbie. I hope he's going to be all right because he's quite vulnerable at times. What would be of concern to me is the fact that he has never really come out of the pop music situation. He's never stepped back from the industry to find out who Robbie Williams is. His life's just been taken over and all those years have just rolled from one year to another. I kind of bailed out after six years, found out who I was again and I'm now happy with myself, but Robbie continued, continued, continued, and I just hope that the right people are surrounding [him] and that [he is] going to be all right in the long term. At some point you kind of get tired of that lifestyle and you've got to step out of that because if you don't you might just end up being a complete head case.'

Although I have suggested that Robbie's post-2000 records do not stand up to his pre-2000 material, I also have to say it is as certain as the day turns into night that he will come back at some point with another purple patch of sheer brilliance. 'I think it's fantastic what Robbie's become,' says Korda Marshall. 'I think he's one of the most exciting, talented artists of the twenty-first century actually, I really think he's up there. I remember seeing the three shows at Knebworth when The Darkness opened and watching Robbie and what he'd become, and I saw him again at the Live 8 concert and he was brilliant. You know natural talent like that when you see it.'

Part of what makes Robbie so compelling is that he has the ability to say something in the press on Saturday that you think seems unfair, cocky or just plain foolish, but then by the time you see him on TV the next day, all is forgiven … because he is so *good*. He always sings live on music shows, he always engages the crowd: it is effortless. In an era when pop bands generally top-and-tail a playback with taped vocals sandwiched between a brief live snap of 'Thanks!', the way Robbie treats television appearances is almost symbolic of the vast gulf between him and pretty much every other mainstream artist in the UK.

Besides, it was hardly likely that his old band-mates in Take That would re-form and match his ticket sales and popularity once again, was it?

BACK WITH THE
BOYS AGAIN

'WE'RE NOT TOTALLY RULING OUT TAKE THAT JUST FOR NOW. WE'VE
TAKEN IT AS FAR AS WE CAN GO AT THE MOMENT BUT THERE MAY BE
MORE TO COME ... YOU KNOW, OUR DREAM IS THAT AFTER FIVE OR TEN
YEARS WE'LL COME BACK AND DO IT ALL AGAIN.'

> *Mark Owen, 13 February 1996, speaking at the*
> *press conference to announce that Take That had split up.*

IN 2004, WITH GARY'S, Mark's and Howard's solo careers stuttering along at best
and finished at worst, the odds of a band reunion must have been about as great as
'the fat dancer out of Take That' (as Liam Gallagher called Robbie) being the country's biggest artist. OK, bad example. But the fact is that until the close of 2005 Take
That were most definitely part of pop music's history.

With the millions of fans around the world still burning the flame, it was inevitable
that questions about a reunion would periodically surface. However, whenever they
did they were quickly extinguished. Howard had been quoted in the press as flatly denying any chance of a reunion, saying, 'Take That could tour without Robbie but we will
never re-form. The rumours aren't true. I see Gary a lot and speak to Mark and Jason
sometimes. Gary is doing really well and Mark just got a new deal. Jason is away travelling and he is difficult to track down. I suppose if somebody wanted us to do a one-
off performance for a million pounds, then, yeah, it's possible – but I doubt it.'

Momentum for a reunion gathered pace in 2003 when the teen pop magazine *Smash
Hits* voted Take That the biggest and best boy band in history, ahead even of Westlife
and Boyzone (both of whom had enjoyed greater statistical chart success). The

175

magazine used coverage as their litmus test, with Take That's twenty-three *Smash Hits* covers beating off all competition. While Madonna enjoyed a cover in 1984 and still justified one in 2001, Take That were clearly the most significant winners in the poll.

However, reunions are only possible if they are commercially viable, and the record-buying public had appeared to vote with their wallets by buying Robbie's solo records in the millions and his former band-mates in only the thousands. Then, in late 2005, ITV1 screened a feature-length documentary entitled *Take That – For the Record*, and launched the programme with a big fanfare; a central London première was organized to promote the corresponding *Greatest Hits* album.

In the programme every member of the band, including Robbie, talked openly and honestly about their career together, about the split, the fans, the That-ers' post-band careers, everything. It was absolutely enthralling to watch (bizarrely voiced over by the same lady who narrated *Celebrity Fit Club*). Made with the cooperation of Simon Cowell's production company, the show culminated in a get-together at a stately home, with the cliffhanger of whether Robbie would turn up or not. He didn't.

Robbie was interviewed as the Brit Award-winning, multi-platinum-selling, Tom Jones-dueting, Knebworth-rousing megastar that he truly is. With that you got a veneer of arrogance, to be expected perhaps, but also a great many insightful comments that showed his more vulnerable side. Particularly poignant were his apologies at the end of the programme to his old band-mates for certain things he'd said and done. Eventually, with many years under the bridge and sitting in the comfort zone of being the country's most successful artist, Robbie retracted many of his nastier comments and persistently highlighted the fun times he'd had with the band. He'd previously said that Gary had come across far better in the post-Take That skirmishes, particularly by his strategy of not being baited when Robbie was at his most withering.

The programme also revealed the warmth between Robbie and Mark: all along, whatever tensions have been evident between Robbie and Gary, Jason or whoever, Mark Owen had always been very complimentary about his friend and the feeling has always been reciprocated. Even at his first solo press conference Robbie had this to say about Mark: 'I'd love to be friendly with Mark Owen. I think everybody needs a little time to see what went on in the past and re-evaluate certain situations. I really miss him, I do.'

Unfortunately, at the end of the day Robbie chose not to turn up, and for many people that said a lot. It was a great shame. Indeed, the moment of the so-called TV 'reveal', when the producers announced to the foursome (who were sitting around a log fire on two sofas) that Robbie was not coming was poignant and quite sad. Even then they did not utter a bad word about Williams. The British public's heart went out to them, four friends waiting for a former cohort, despite everything that had been said and done. And perhaps, with the benefit of hindsight, that moment of genuine humility on their part was when the public's allegiance shifted from Robbie to Take That.

To be fair, Robbie was far from antagonistic. Robbie said Howard was 'never anything but nice', that Mark was 'a genius', that Jason was 'a lovely man' and that Gary was 'an amazing songwriter with an amazing voice. I apologize for saying you weren't, I had my head up my arse.' Fooling us with some sarcasm, Robbie then said of Gary's devoted family life and children, 'Fourteen Brits! Fuck off! … In all seriousness, I would swap everything that I have for that.' Some people asked if Robbie meant it … it doesn't matter, he still had the balls to say it.

Despite some fairly venomous comments between Robbie and Nigel, the latter had some fascinating things to say. Michael Metcalf of GMTV reinforces the general consensus that Nigel was absolutely key to Take That's success. 'I think they have a lot of respect for him, no matter what the press have said over the years. I've got a lot of time for him, I think he did a great job for them. He was always a really nice guy. I think it's that Manchester/northern thing. He's very down to earth but he knows his artists and he knows what's best for them.'

A monologue from Jason in his Jeep was tinged with sadness, not least when he admitted that he struggled to sleep and was often 'willing myself to fail'. It wasn't only the public who watched fascinated. The music industry was buzzing with talk of the show the next morning, as Brian Harvey said to me: 'After watching that documentary, I really think Howard comes across very well. Mark comes across as "butter wouldn't melt in his mouth", but you know what? He is actually like that! He's a lovely man. It was such a rarity to see nice people talking about their experiences – I came away with the conclusion that they were a fucking good bunch of geezers. I thought it was shame from the public's point of view that Robbie didn't turn up, but I suppose he had his reasons.

'A lot of years have gone by and everyone has grown up in both bands, but watching that show there were so many similarities. There's always a character in the band who kind of gets looked at as the front man, even though they are not necessarily the songwriter – in Take That it was Robbie and in East 17 that was me. Further down the line, though, the way Take That started, the way they ended, the problems they had after the group, it all sounded so familiar.'

'THE PUBLIC'S ALLEGIANCE SHIFTED FROM ROBBIE TO TAKE THAT.'

The next day it wasn't just the music business that was fired up about Take That – every office, factory, radio station, student … *everybody* was talking about the programme. Viewing figures were way over 6 million. Take That's place in the nation's hearts, it seemed, was still treasured. They weren't just a throwback from a former decade. It was precisely this catalyst that led to the exciting news nine days later that the four members of Take That – excluding Robbie – were re-forming for a tour. Given that it was only a couple of years previously that Gary had shut down his website and

Mark Owen's solo career repeatedly failed to take off, despite him winning *Celebrity Big Brother*, it was all the more remarkable what happened once the announcement had been made … *Britain went Take That mad.*

How had the band come to re-form? They'd been friends for years, of course, and the ITV documentary was not a reconciliation for the four members other than Robbie, because they'd never really fallen out. However, they later revealed that after the programme had been filmed three of them went out for a night together to talk about the rabid reaction by the public: 'Me, Gary and Howard went out for a drink,' explained Mark in *Q*, 'and we had a couple of drinks and we thought, "We can do it!" Basically we were a bit slopped up and we phoned Jay, I think he was at a wedding, and we said, "Jay, Jay, we've got this brilliant idea. Come back!" So he came back from the wedding at two in the morning, we went round to Gary's house and we stayed up till six, envisioning it, getting all really excited. Then we went home and slept, and then obviously when you wake up it was like, "What have we decided to do?"'

Their trepidation is understandable. It is easy to say now that *of course* the band would sell out venues, but the sheer size of the tour they announced – massive arenas – was a huge gamble. Many in the industry wondered if the band would be playing to medium-sized venues, 2,000 or so people, maybe the 4,000-capacity Brixton Academy or similar at best. Or worse, what if the public did not react well and they were forced to cancel shows or downgrade them to little more than a chicken-in-a-basket tribute act? There had been a recent spate of Eighties re-formation tours and even a TV show, but these rarely lifted the contributors out of the pure nostalgia circuit.

The eight venues planned were a shock to say the least: two nights at Birmingham's NEC, two nights at the MEN in Manchester, two nights at Wembley Arena, as well as one-night shows in more arena sheds in Newcastle, Glasgow, Sheffield, Dublin and Belfast. This was tens of thousands of tickets. Many believed that Take That were quite possibly on the verge of one of the most humiliating comeback anti-climaxes in pop history.

They were completely and unreservedly wrong.

What is more, no one knew what was coming next.

'WE WANT TO SEE THEM TOUR.'

The tickets sold out fast, faster than any other act in the whole of 2005. All of them went in thirty minutes. Promoters were forced to add a further fifteen dates due to the

incredible demand. But not just a few more arenas. The brand-new Wembley Stadium, whose capacity would be about 80,000; Cardiff Millennium Stadium, so recently filled by tens of thousands of Foo Fighters fans; the list went on. In a word, it was awesome. At least these enormous shows might take longer to sell out. They did – but it still only it took six hours.

Nigel Hassler, who had booked early shows for Take That, was now one of the country's highest-profile agents at Helter Skelter Agency, and his insider view on the reformation tour is enlightening. 'When it was initially booked, it was just an arena tour with room to expand, depending on demand. However, everybody was taken back by the speed and the success of the ticket sales. To sell out that many nights at Wembley arena, close to 70,000 tickets, more in Manchester … The Red Hot Chili Peppers would sell very quickly; Madonna sells very quickly; the Rolling Stones sell very quickly too; but there is only one artist who can sell that sort of volume quicker than these Take That shows … and that's Robbie Williams.'

Despite this, before the dates were confirmed, not every agent in the country was convinced. 'Various promoters and agents discussed it,' recalls Nigel Hassler, 'and as far as I am aware one thought it would do OK and another person didn't fancy it at all. I think the reason a lot of my peers thought it might not do the business was because Robbie wasn't involved, I think that was the question mark, but it doesn't seem to have made any difference at all. So you can imagine everyone's surprise when the arena dates sold out, then the stadium shows were added and they sold out just as quickly. It's phenomenal business.'

He puts a lot of the credit on the ITV1 documentary: 'That TV show had a massive impact. I think for a lot of people it brought back fond memories of how good the songs were and the good times they had with Take That, and according to the incredible ticket sales, people thought, *We want to see them tour*.'

Brian Harvey of East 17 understands perfectly well what an exciting yet weird experience this would be, diving straight into the cauldron once again: 'It must be mad. It must feel like a real trip down memory lane. It must feel good, help your confidence and your self-esteem. At the same time, it must be a little strange for them because they're a lot older now and your minds change as you get older and you mature.'

Ben from Phats & Small and Four Story thinks the band's live reputation is a large factor in the success of these dates: 'Talking to Take That during those dates in 1995 when my band Benz supported them, it was clear that they understood that what to them was just another show, for the fans on that night they might have built their entire year around it. They were very aware of that. People love music because it is escapism and they were very tuned in to their fans and what was needed. They were amazing at having 18,000 people in a room and making individuals feel like they were speaking personally to them. That's what all great bands can do. Take That effortlessly made that connection. They appreciated what their music did, they appreciated their fans, they talked openly about them backstage, about what they meant, not just when the press were there.'

Boyzone's Shane Lynch was delighted to hear the news; speaking in 2006 he told me: 'I still have a high regard for Take That and I was genuinely quite excited, to be honest. I think they were an amazing group. When I actually got into the same profession as them, I had the utmost respect for them. I think it's amazing, I'm really jealous that they're getting back together. I would absolutely love to do it!' (Shane and the rest of Boyzone reunited for a huge series of arena shows themselves in 2008 and 2009.)

Inevitably, following the tour and TV show, the band's scheduled greatest hits album *Never Forget* hit No. 2 and quickly approached a million sales. Intriguingly, it contained a new track, entitled 'Today I've Lost You', which was written in 1995 and was originally planned to be the follow-up to 'Back for Good'. This, naturally, led to wild rumours about new material being written.

After the reunion was announced, Take That went in to GMTV and Michael Metcalf was pleased to see little had changed: 'The thing that always struck me when I met them was that they always seemed to be having a good time. When you meet some bands, you think, *Bloody hell, if it's this much hard work for you, why do you do it?* Take That always seemed to be having a good time together. They came across as being mates, whereas sometimes you'd meet bands who you know are never going to see each other out of the studio.

'Also, it makes a difference to the people working in TV if a band is enjoying themselves and are nice people. In my job I work with lots of bands and quite often you think, *Oh dear, I'm not looking forward to tomorrow's work.* With Take That you only ever think, *Oh great, it's going to be a good morning.* When they came in for us to talk about the reunion, the buzz within GMTV was incredible. I had so many people asking me if they could come down and see them. We had people hanging around the corridors to see them and wanting photographs with them, it was crazy. In the end, I said to Nigel Martin-Smith, "We've got a number of staff who are massive fans. Is there any chance they could say hello?" Both Nigel and the band said, "No problem, we'd love to see them," and they stood and chatted to people from GMTV and didn't appear to be rushed, they took ages with them. It was a lovely morning's work.'

Once the shows sold out, the press was bombarded with news stories and updates: Lulu would be performing, Robbie wouldn't be singing at the final Wembley Stadium show, Will Young would like to, Mylene Klass was also mentioned, the band were seen holed up in LA watching high-profile gigs to research ideas for what would undoubt-edly be an incredible show … Suddenly, almost without warning, we were all right back in the thick of Take That mania.

'TAKE THAT ALWAYS SEEMED TO BE HAVING A GOOD TIME TOGETHER.'

Nigel Hassler is a realist, and prior to the release of the band's comeback album was very balanced about the prospects for success: 'Will it survive, will [the hype] con-tinue? I think a lot will be down to the quality of any new record they may release. The tour sales succeeded partly because there was an element of the nostalgia factor, but whether people will come back year in and year out will depend on the quality of the record.'

Korda Marshall, the man who signed the cheque for the band's first major record deal, was perhaps best placed to have the closing comment on the shocking scale of the

first reunion tour. Speaking to the author in 2005, he said, 'Culturally and commercially, I think Take That had a great run at the time for what they were doing. I think they brought a lot of entertainment and enjoyment to a lot of people, especially a lot of females. It's been a really positive story, the whole Take That tale, and it's lovely that they are getting back together. I think the interest on the back of the TV programme and for the tour is testament to the strength of the songs and the strength of them as a band. They could always put their tongues in their cheeks and get on with it; they knew they weren't Oasis or a so-called "credible" band, they were out to entertain and have fun and to be entertainers. That's what they did, and they did it brilliantly. Long may that continue.'

BACK FOR GOOD

'YOU CHANGE YOUR MIND OVER DECISIONS LIKE THIS EVERY DAY ... IT SHOULD BRING BACK SOME HAPPY MEMORIES AND BE A GREAT NIGHT OUT. AND THAT'LL BE THE MAX OF IT.'

Mark Owen, speaking in early 2006 about
Take That's forthcoming reunion tour.

WHEN ROBBIE WILLIAMS LIFTED ONE of his fifteen Brit Awards in the air in 1997 and said, 'I was always the talented member of the band,' his victory, it seemed, was complete. Multi-million-selling, critically acclaimed, universally adored and with a batch of classic songs already in his solo catalogue, his status was assured. If, at that point, you'd have suggested that ten years to the day Robbie would be in rehab with his most recent album viciously panned and touring commitments cancelled, while a day later his former band-mates were picking up their own Brit Award, you would have been thought at best fanciful, at worst deluded.

But it happened.

At the time of writing, Take That are bigger than Robbie Williams.

They have made the biggest comeback in pop history.

Bar none.

The first hardback edition of this book was published in the same week that Take That began their comeback tour. At that point, despite the staggering ticket sales, it was still unclear whether this was a night out of choice for a nation of office parties or a bona fide return to form. That it was the latter was the undoubted musical success story of 2006 ... and possibly of the decade.

The signs were good as the New Year of 2006 broke. The ITV1 documentary that had kicked off the whole reunion tour when it was aired the previous October, was nominated for the prestigious Rose d'Or. Within hours of going on sale, all the shows sold out. By February a seat for a Take That show was like a Willy Wonka golden ticket.

The weeks leading up to the tour were not without incident, and with the eyes of the world's media focused firmly on the returning TT circus we were treated to ludicrous details of their activities on an almost daily basis. After jovial comments from the more 'mature' band members about hiring body doubles to perform the more tricky dance manoeuvres, their modesty was only half-rooted in jest, it seemed. Only a few days before the opening show in Newcastle, Jason Orange was feared to have torn a ligament in his leg while rehearsing a particularly difficult dance routine. At first, the rumours suggested that his hamstring had been heard to 'pop' – usually a sign of a tear or rip – and that he was out of the entire tour. With just three of the original five left, this would have cast serious doubts on the validity of the project.

'THE BOYS AREN'T AS YOUNG AS THEY USED TO BE.'

He was rushed straight to a physiotherapist who explained that the damage was far less than at first feared and that, with intensive treatment, the tour was still a possibility. The normal recuperation time for an injury such as this would be eight weeks; Jason astounded everyone by turning up at rehearsal only one week later. The *Sun* reported a source close to the band as saying, 'The boys aren't as young as they used to be, and they are very conscious of the fact they have ageing muscles. The slightest hint of a niggle and it's panic stations. They don't want to get injured and put themselves out of action close to the beginning of the tour.'

Jason seemed remarkably unperturbed about the whole injury scare. He even turned up for one rehearsal in a codpiece and matching studded jacket, in a jokey throwback to their former 'Do What You Like' days. Thankfully, although the other three enjoyed the practical joke, they did not decide to rekindle the look for the new shows. Quite how father-of-two Gary Barlow would have felt in a leather S&M outfit this time is a matter for speculation (to be fair, he was looking very trim and had been on a strict diet, broken only on the tour's first night by a treat of roast beef, Yorkshire pudding and apple pie). Mark, famous for his 'Junkie's Baddy Powder' crop-tops and skimpy out-fits, looked as if he may have only put on a few ounces since his younger days, but even he was dressing somewhat more demurely. 'Julia Roberts has a bum double, so maybe I can get one too, then I can wear the chaps again.'

Of course, one of the hot topics of conversation in the months leading up to the tour was whether Robbie Williams would be rejoining his old pals on stage. Robbie respectfully said he was too busy and that the audience did not want to see him, it was all about the four in Take That. The band said they had no plans to invite him on stage for the whole tour. However, fans and the media alike read a multitude of meanings into every word that was spoken on the subject. There was speculation that guest singers would appear instead, such as Will Young, Charlotte Church and Lulu (who at one point said she was sure she could convince Robbie to join the shows). Even Sir Elton John chipped into the speculation, urging Robbie to rejoin the band and 'let it go, it doesn't matter, get the monkey off your back'.

Would the comeback have been better with Robbie on stage?

No.

There can be no doubt that the first comeback tour benefited hugely from Robbie not being involved. Somehow, his absence seemed to stamp the foursome as the 'gen-

uine' Take That line-up. Robbie's high-profile career, drug and alcohol problems had distanced him from TT so much that it was almost hard to recall him as a member. Besides, it seemed unthinkable to see him on stage alongside his four former band-mates. It just would not have worked. Even the talk of him turning up for 'Relight My Fire' was implausible. The entire package would have been confused, ambiguous, complicated. 'The band did their last big tour as a four-piece,' said a spokesman, 'so they don't think Robbie will really be missed this time round.' Indeed.

'HIS ABSENCE SEEMED TO STAMP THE FOURSOME AS THE "GENUINE" TAKE THAT LINE-UP.'

Besides, why should TT ask him? Why should they care? Yes, they were friends, and even Gary implied that the old problems were all water under the bridge, but – in the author's opinion – TT did exactly the right thing by going on stage without him. Instead, using hologram footage of him for 'Could It Be Magic?' as a cheeky nod to their past was an ideal and clever diversion.

The media reported almost daily on the 'Will he, won't he?' saga.

Ultimately, he didn't.

Support acts the Sugababes and Beverly Knight had a difficult task on their hands, as the show was always going to be about Take That (there were rumours backstage that the Sugababes and Gary did not get on). One thing that was not in doubt was the boys' work ethic – famed within the industry – as they rehearsed every day for weeks before the opening night.

Their meticulous preparation went deeper than that. Prior to the rehearsals, the boys had all travelled to Las Vegas for inspiration for their stage show, and the glitzy influence of the Nevada strip was obvious for all to see (although Gary fell asleep during Celine Dion's show). What the public didn't know until later was that, even as the Newcastle Arena was filling up for the opening night on 23 April, Jason was having last-minute doubts, even contemplating leaving the venue and not playing the show. Clearly his comments in the documentary about failing and his inner turmoil still plagued him, but it is perhaps a sign of his modesty and famed down-to-earth nature that even with the nation bowing down to his band's return he was still anxious about producing the goods. 'Just before we went on stage I was standing behind the curtain wondering what the hell I was doing.' He told the other three, who were understand-ably a little concerned, but thankfully they talked him around! He later said he'd just 'got used to being anonymous', so to be thrust back into the spotlight again was a big leap for him.

The show was lavish, exciting, exacting in detail and preparation. The band's costumes veered from Oscar Wilde-esque frills, to Beatles suits, to casual shirts and circus costume (inspired by seeing Cirque du Soleil in Vegas). One obvious highlight was the Tango version of 'It Only Takes a Minute' – reworked because the boys felt the original pop version was simply too young; 'Could It Be Magic?' featured an intro courtesy of Robbie Williams, appearing as that hologram; 'Back for Good' came complete with rainstorms and no doubt a nervous breakdown for the stage electrician; 'Babe' was

performed simply and was huge; the 'Making of a Boy Band' segue was very clever, neatly diluting any criticism they may have faced for re-forming in their mid-thirties; and the monumental show closer, 'Never Forget', was an apt and triumphant way to climax the set.

At one stage there were nearly thirty other dancers and acrobats on stage, but this never distracted from the band, even when the scantily clad females threatened to give the entire show a definite risqué feel – the outrageous film *Moulin Rouge* was a big influence on the set and visuals. No expense was spared. Over the course of twenty-six dates at the country's biggest arenas – including six nights at Wembley Arena and five at Birmingham NEC – the UK fell in love with Take That all over again.

Gary later said it was the best tour he had ever done.

Not everyone agreed with the almost universal acclaim for the shows. East 17's Tony Mortimer rekindled some of the former rivalry by slating the TT tour: 'They are just

a trumped-up Village People tribute band. They covered Barry Manilow!' Implying that the speculation about Robbie appearing on tour had been a deliberate ploy to shift tickets, he said, 'Would there be that much interest in Take That if they hadn't played the Robbie card?' He went on to say that Gary's kids 'might have daddy issues' because of the TT singer's dancing ability (unlikely, given that they'd also see him headlining the country's biggest arenas and stadiums to thousands of adoring fans … just a thought).

'I'M JUST STUNNED THAT PEOPLE STILL WANT TO SEE US AND STILL CARE.'

Reflecting on the shows themselves, the band was ecstatic. 'I'm euphoric,' said Mark. 'I didn't in a million years expect [this]. It's turned my world upside down. It's all good.' Howard concurred, saying, 'What a buzz! I'd forgotten what it was like. I'm just stunned that people still want to see us and still care.'

'I was really tired afterwards,' said Jason after the tour. 'My bones felt shattered. It's so much harder now!' He also admitted that he hadn't yet invited any family or friends to the gigs because he was still finding it hard to handle. Half a million people watched the thirty-one-date sell-out tour; Lulu did not play the European dates, saying, 'They're adorable, but no!' (One terrible afternote to that monumental first TT gig in ten years was that a pregnant woman at the show unexpectedly went into labour at the concert and lost her baby, despite the best attentions of paramedics at the venue. The band issued a statement sending their condolences.)

By the time the band left the Wembley Arena stage for the last night of the tour, the hype and expectancy for the next chapter in the TT story was rabid. In keeping with the ingenious way the entire comeback had been organized, TT had already planted the seed. Cleverly, even before the tour had opened, it was announced that Take That had signed a record deal with Polydor – not for reissues either, but based on demos of new material the band had already recorded. The advance was rumoured to be in the region of £3 million. Despite their earlier warnings that the comeback was only meant to be temporary, this news confirmed that TT were very much back for, er, good. Polydor Co-President David Joseph told the press, 'When we met them, it quickly became clear their best songs and albums are yet to come.' Hyperbole, perhaps, but events since that statement have proved him correct. Although rumours initially suggested that progress was slow, in fact the band produced enough new material for three albums.

Understandably, in the wake of pop's biggest-ever comeback, other bands from the same era decided to re-emerge and play some shows. East 17 were one of the first out of the blocks, some nine years after their original demise – their comeback only extended to one show at London's Shepherds Bush Empire in May 2006; All Saints came back with a new album and looked fantastic – the opening single 'Rock Steady' was beautifully produced with a suitably expensive video, but the snappy follow-up single, 'Chick Fit', and corresponding album failed to re-ignite the public's interest; then, most significantly of all perhaps, Boyzone refused to deny rumours in early 2007 that they were about to reunite but, as mentioned, did exactly that later in the year.

Away from the stage, 2006 was a hectic year for Take That. The most important day of Mark Owen's year arrived in August with the birth of his first-born child with his partner Emma Macdonald, Elwood Jack. Emma thought of the name for their son and it won the day over Mark's suggestions of Bowie and Dylan! (Elwood is actually the name of one of the Blues Brothers.) He took time away from the intense studio sessions to be with his partner and child – a sign that this time around the band's priorities about balancing their lives and careers were more considered. Mark later announced that he and Emma planned to get married some time soon.

Behind the scenes, the band had previously parted ways with their manager Nigel Martin-Smith, who was furious about the development and was heavily critical of them. The band's new manager was Jonathan Wild. The repercussions of former glory days were still being felt between Nigel Martin-Smith and Robbie too. Martin-Smith launched legal action about a track called 'The Nineties' whose lyrics appeared to be a vitriolic tirade against him (after legal proceedings, Robbie agreed to pay undisclosed damages to Martin-Smith and said via his lawyer that 'he did not intend these lyrics to be taken at face value and … did not intend to allege that Nigel Martin-Smith has ever stolen funds from Take That or anyone'. Further, prior to the release of his next solo album, the lyrics themselves were altered after legal discussion.)

One shocking fact that emerged from the press frenzy surrounding the comeback tour was that Gary had been caught up in the terrible terrorist attacks in London on 7 July 2005. It transpired that he was actually on a train running alongside another train that exploded and was even thrown to the ground by the force of the bomb. When he got to his feet, he looked across and saw a train with its roof and side ripped off. He saw dead bodies strewn across the exposed seats and even counted seven corpses. Clearly traumatized by the shocking near-death experience, Gary was quoted on contactmusic.com saying, 'I began to understand how lucky I had been. I made it home on adrenaline, I guess, and for the next three hours I was glued to the news. I don't know why there or why then, but I began to cry in the shower. Thank God I'm still here. I can't stop kissing my children. I have never been so happy to be alive.'

Gary also spoke with refreshing honesty about his state of mind after the demise of TT and then his own muted solo career. He spoke of feeling depressed and revealed that he gorged on food and smoked cannabis. His own autobiography, *My Take*, was published in 2006 and not surprisingly became a best-seller.

On the ITV1 documentary, viewers had been offered a glimpse inside Gary's palatial Cheshire mansion, crammed full of expensive antiques and valuables. By October 2006, however, he and his family had decided to move to London and put Delamere Manor up for sale. Going from a cavernous country mansion to a (no doubt beautiful) London house was a big change in lifestyle, but the Barlows threw themselves into it, auctioning off chests full of more than sixty possessions, including a Versace bedspread, a pair of urns, a Grecian-style stool and a collection of paintings. In suitably inappropriate detail (hypocritically repeated here), the media declared the items fetched just over £11,000. Gary later admitted that the house was 'full of clutter' and the expensive antiques and furniture were really a result of not knowing what else to do with his reported fortune of over £25 million.

The new rash of interviews also revealed how Jason had tried and failed to get a role in the soap *Coronation Street* after the band's original split. He told *Attitude*, 'They seemed really keen but nothing came of it. I was gutted but I realized that at the time I just wasn't in the right frame of mind to be a soap person, and they [the producers]

recognized that.' He also said he'd gone back to college and studied psychology, biology, history and English, travelled a bit and kept a low profile, 'a bit of hanging on the club scene, drinking more than I wanted to – but I was never comfortable doing it'.

The first glimpse of new Take That material came with the October 2006 DVD release *The Ultimate Tour – Live in Manchester*, which featured live footage of the sell-out tour as well as very revealing behind-the-scenes clips and a bonus CD with further snippets. This was the appetizer, however, for the forthcoming and hugely anticipated first new TT single in a decade. Released in late November 2006, 'Patience' was a masterful song, its gentle refrain and controlled falsetto making it a clear relation to the classic 'Back for Good'. Given that the band's last release ten years previously had been a Bee Gees cover, this original new single was a beauty … although the band themselves were initially surprised when the record company heard it and insisted on that track being the first single.

'"PATIENCE" WAS A MASTERFUL SONG.'

The promo video was stylish and moody, filmed in the volcano-blackened landscapes of Reykjavik in Iceland. The band's choice of director for the clip was intriguing – David Mould, who had an impressive track record of working with slightly more 'alternative' bands such as The Magic Numbers, Radiohead and Doves. The clips were taken in four different locations as each band member heads towards a meet with his colleagues. Gary said he didn't know the story-line but 'just wanted to go to Iceland!'.

The new album, entitled *Beautiful World*, was released one week after 'Patience', on 27 November. It was packaged luxuriously, with the group's image and style living up to their newly christened status as 'the world's biggest man-band'. Here was a boy band in their mid-to-late thirties, with children, wives, a few more wrinkles, a worldly disposition and a fan-base that had grown older with them. Previous comebacks by boy bands never had the same credibility and were always seen as boys trying to be men. He's put on a lot weight … Is that a wig? … They still don't write the songs … but with Take That, they actually looked *better* this time around. There was less squeaky-clean purity, less styling (though they were no less stylish) and more cool. There was more substance too – the liner notes revealed that the industry rumours were true, and the entire band had shared writing and vocal duties (writing credits stated 'All tracks written by Take That/John Shanks').

The ideas for the new record came from a variety of inspirations: 'We had many a conversation about the tone and style of what Take That should become in this new chapter,' Jason told *Attitude* magazine. 'The Beatles, ELO and the Eagles [were thrown] into the equation, music we all grew up listening to.'

You could tell – the Eighties sounds of opener 'Reach Out' did not stop it from being a stand-out track, a real feel-good start to the record; slices of ELO and A-Ha were strewn over 'Beautiful World', with the sophisticated single 'Patience' sandwiched in between; Howard's vocals were showcased too, perhaps to best effect on 'Mancunian Way'; Mark's vocals sounded cheeky – whereas previously his solo material had been more rock-oriented – while Gary's vocal was pure class, especially on songs such as 'Like I Never Loved You at All' and the hidden track. It was a breathtaking batch of pop, ballads, soft rock, all seamlessly produced. By way of reinforcing the tour dates and their huge popularity, Take That had delivered the ideal record and, without a doubt, their best album to date.

Most surprising of all was the last track (aside from the hidden song), 'Wooden Boat'. Jason's lead vocal was astounding – had Damien Rice released this, the critics would have been fawning. Jason was so thrilled to have the lead vocal he was reported to have cried when they recorded the song in a Los Angeles studio. 'I've waited fifteen years for this moment,' he later said. 'It was actually the lads that suggested I record it.' Having been totally out of the business for ten years since the split, he was the band member who found returning to the spotlight the biggest culture shock.

'SUDDENLY WE WERE LISTENING TO A BAND WHO WERE MORE THAN JUST GARY BARLOW, WHO WERE ALL SINGING, ALL-DANCING AND CLEARLY MULTI-TALENTED.'

Part of the reason for Take That's comeback becoming so huge so quickly was that the album was a genuinely great record. Further, whether by deliberate design or sincere magnanimity between friends, the decision to showcase both Howard and Jason's lead vocals on certain songs was a master-stroke. Suddenly we were listening to a band who were more than just Gary Barlow, who were all singing, all-dancing and clearly multi-talented. The stamp of authenticity and quality that this four-way split on vocals created cannot be underestimated.

The first week of December 2006 was a milestone in Take That history – both their single and album were at No. 1. This took their chart tally at that point to nine No. 1 singles and four chart-topping albums. The double success marked the start of a remarkable dominance of both charts … and with download and European stats added, this meant the single was No. 1 in five separate charts at the same time, a world first.

That week also saw the screening of *An Audience with Take That*, a traditional ITV honour reserved for only the most revered of artists (and an achievement that was frankly an absurd impossibility only eighteen months previously). Gary later admitted that the rehearsal went so well that he was convinced the actual filming would be a disaster! The band broke with tradition and recorded the show totally live (for the first time in the programme's forty-episode history) in front of a star-studded audience including Peter Kay, members of Girls Aloud and ex-Spice Girl Mel C. Lulu and Jason scotched once and for all rumours of a tryst, Mark kept texting the show himself from the stage for 'Babe' to be sung, Howard seemed ecstatic, while Gary seemed completely relaxed, chatting to the celebs and effectively compering the evening. They looked like a *team*. The most staggering fact for the night was that 'Back for Good' has been covered eighty-nine times! With their witty asides and relaxed manner, the band somehow turned the whole evening into a nostalgia trip it was OK to indulge in, yet at the same time made it feel completely fresh and current … and the row after row of glassy-eyed celeb women spoke volumes for the band's renewed sex appeal. As one observer said, 'being a man suits Gary Barlow much better than being a boy' (this was confirmed when he won 'Best Music Personality Hairstyle' in late 2007, an award previously the preserve of Mark Owen).

They also appeared on *Parkinson*, home of the so-called chat-show king. The boys were clearly delighted to be invited on, as the programme is a British TV institution and appearances are highly prized. The boys sang 'Patience' and, for the first time, Gary looked a little more portly than his earlier slimline self. Parky revealed audience members had been queuing up all day and the screams from the That-ers in the crowd verified that! When asked about the success of the tour, Gary said, 'It was so unexpected, it wasn't a big plan drawn up, we just sort of followed it as we've gone along … and [look] how faithful our fans are!'

Talk inevitably turned to Robbie, and Howard admitted that the break-up 'affected me more than the others [he went to live with his mum]. Robbie is an amazing guy …' at which point there was a notable absence of cheers from the audience. Gary – looking as relaxed as he has ever been in the public eye – added with a grin that he had 'no problem with [Robbie] singing the second verse', to a rousing cheer. Elsewhere in TV-land, one of the biggest shows is *X Factor*, so it was enthralling to see Take That make a guest appearance to sing alongside finalist (and eventual winner) Leona Lewis; they were up against cheeky chappy (oh no, not another one …) Ray Quinn.

Another part of the promotion for the new album saw the band treat 300 very lucky fans to an intimate gig at the legendary Abbey Road Studios, made famous by The

Beatles and the world's best-known pedestrian crossing. Suitably, they rounded off their set with a Beatles medley – Gary has always acknowledged how much of an influence the Fab Four have been on his songwriting.

With ticket sales outstripping any other act in the UK and the album selling faster than any other record of 2006, it was only a matter of time before the band started scooping awards too. First up was the Vodafone Live Music Awards in October, where they won 'Best Live Return'; at the Grosvenor Hotel for the *Q* Music Awards, the band – featured on that magazine's front cover in late 2006 – scooped the 'Idol' Award, only to be berated by the Arctic Monkeys' lead singer Alex Turner as 'bollocks' and taunted by the admittedly ultra-witty Noel Gallagher; BBC Radio 2 listeners caused a few surprises by voting TT into their Top 5 of the 'Best British Bands' survey; and most superficially yet equally importantly, *New Woman* magazine readers voted Take That 'the Hottest Hunk [*sic*] in the World', which was at best an oddity and at worst a blatant mistruth. Individuals below them included Brad Pitt, Johnny Depp and, most notably, down in a relatively lowly ninth place, Robbie Williams.

However, it was February 2007's Brit Awards that everyone was looking to for a final endorsement of the band's colossal comeback. When the nominations were announced, most observers were actually mystified by the disappointing sole nod to the boys (bizarrely not even 'Best Live' category), but on the night they scooped 'Best

British Single' for 'Patience'. Notably, although other acts won more awards, the head-lines the next day were all about Take That's triumph.

The controversial comedian Russell Brand ruffled quite a few feathers presenting the Brits, with jokes about friendly-fire deaths and the Queen's private parts which caused a storm of criticism. However, his introduction of Take That's live performance was genius and sums up the story – now and then: 'The story of Robbie Williams and Take That is a power struggle of Shakespearian proportions in its twists and complexity. First he left Take That and went fat, then he was friends with Oasis and all cool, then Howard and Jason went camping for a decade while Mark won *Big Brother*, now Rob-bie is in rehab and they're the Kings of Showbiz. By the end of the week Robbie will probably be Prime Minister and they will all be falsely imprisoned as shoe bombers.' (Mark later said he felt Robbie was 'being mocked' by these jokes, which made him 'feel bad'.)

Gary almost didn't make the ceremony, as he was unaware the venue had changed since he last attended the event in the mid-Nineties! Fortunately, although he started driving to Alexandra Palace, he realized his mistake and made it to Earls Court in time. Backstage, everyone wanted to meet the band. Korda Marshall, by then Man-aging Director of Warners but previously the man who had signed the band to their first record deal at RCA, was there: 'I bumped into Mark at the Brits. He'd hurt his hand so we gave each other a hug. They were rehearsing and, not surprisingly, were being the consummate professionals, accomplished at meet-and-greet, always have been. Mark still looked 16! He had a smile from ear to ear. They were lovely, as always.'

The band appeared genuinely moved by the award, hailed by the voice-over as 'the most spectacular comeback in the Brits' twenty-seven-year history'. Gary and Mark were stunned, and Howard said 'Happy Birthday!' to his daughter Lola, but the moment will be remembered for Jason's impassioned speech to his father Tony, who was in the audience as his guest. Showing that second time around they are all more mature and comfortable with their celebrity, he said, 'The first time Take That hap-pened, I cut my dad out of the picture for whatever reason. But me dad's here tonight. Dad, I love you.' Tony Orange later revealed that he was overcome with emotion and understandably ecstatic to see this rift resolved after all these years. After the show Gary was transparently delighted with the award, telling the media, 'If we are gonna hit the heights, this is it. Tonight is as high as we can get. It's incredible.'

A few more cynical observers claimed TT had 'snubbed' Robbie – the day before the Brits (Rob's 33rd birthday) he had checked into an American rehab clinic for treatment for a reported dependency on prescription drugs. On the contrary, Gary and Mark in particular were eager to send their sympathies to their former band-mate: 'There are some people who will never be happy,' said Gary, 'and I fear Robbie will be one of them.' Elsewhere, he said if he had personally gone into rehab he'd have kept the matter private, which led to some journalists suggesting he was implying it should have been kept quiet – hence the accusations of a 'snub'.

Mark was clearly not distancing himself from his old pal, saying, 'I'm so worried about him. I'm gutted and devastated things have ended up like this. I think he should

come back to the UK. When I heard about him checking into rehab I felt really sad – I just want him to get happy again. I'll do anything I can to help him. If he wants me to see him, I'll be straight on that plane.'

So TT had done no such snub, but Robbie's admission to rehab was the nadir of a very difficult year for the star. The start came with the release of the opening single – the title track – from his 2006 album, *Rudebox*. I actually loved the single – it was audacious, funny and addictive – but I was in a relatively small minority as both the press and public pretty much shunned both the song and the accompanying video. For me, any track that has the lyric, 'TK Maxx costs less,' deserves critical acclaim. Liam Gallagher disagreed, calling it 'dog s**t'.

'IF HE WANTS ME TO SEE HIM, I'LL BE STRAIGHT ON THAT PLANE.'

Gary Barlow did not enjoy the track, although his criticism was nowhere near as barbed as his former band-mate's previous verbal volleys. When pushed on his opinion of the derided song, Gary was almost diplomatic. 'Do I like "Rudebox"? If I'm honest, I prefer classic Robbie, and I don't think of "Rudebox" as a classic Robbie song.'

Some observers suggested Robbie was suffering a 'Take That backlash', that the public were so pleased to see TT back that they were not receptive to new Robbie material. The role of underdog had perhaps been reversed. This seems unlikely, although there was a genuine tidal wave of affection and warmth for the band in the papers as well as on the streets. Sadly, as record sales will verify, the same could not be said for Robbie. Most poignantly, although *Rudebox* made it to No. 1 in the album charts, it was knocked off the top spot by Robbie's former cohorts with the multi-million-selling *Beautiful World*. There couldn't have been a starker contrast in fortunes. Worse was to come. Later reports suggested unsold copies of *Rudebox* were being recycled in China and used to resurface roads.

How had it come to this? Speaking musically, the reason *Rudebox* struggled was that it was by far Robbie's worst album. As mentioned earlier, his solo albums had stuttered a little creatively since the golden era of 'Millennium', 'No Regrets' *et al* – *Rudebox* was a poor record, brave in its intentions but limited in its achievements.

Before the 2006 tour Robbie had issued a statement to the press that he planned to quit touring after these dates, 'at least for a long time'; when events overtook him, he never even completed the tour. When the news broke that Robbie had cancelled dates on his tour, citing exhaustion, concern grew for his well-being. Again Gary was equally magnanimous (given Robbie's previous vitriolic response to his misfortunes), instead saying, 'I'd hate to see him go through what I've been through. I don't know if he'd come out the other end.'

Regardless of Robbie's predicament, the Take That juggernaut showed no sign of stopping. The question in relation to their former band-mate now was, 'Did Robbie need Take That to relaunch his career?', not the other way around. The second single was a very odd choice – *Beautiful World*'s weakest track, 'Shine'. The video was very glitzy and reinforced the Vegas feel, with help from Scissor Sisters' stylist Jonny Blue Eyes. However, the song struggled to sound anything other than an ELO tribute played by the Scissor Sisters. Still, this author was again in the minority and it smashed its way to No. 1 in the charts in March 2007. This was their tenth chart-topper – only The Beatles, Elvis, Sir Cliff, Westlife, The Shadows and Madonna have enjoyed more No. 1s.

THE CIRCUS
COMES TO TOWN

GIVEN THAT THE BAND HAD, by now, revealed they were all initially reluctant to re-form, the degree of success of this comeback album and tour must have astounded them. With *Beautiful World* staying high in the charts for month after month after month – and even returning to the top spot four months after its initial release, fuelled by the band's Brit success and 'Shine' being at No. 1 – Take That somehow seemed to have become a permanent fixture in the charts. The staggering success of the new album was perhaps even more impressive given that they actually only released a modest two singles from the record.

Their appearance at the Concert for Diana in July 2007 was followed by yet another hit song. Such was the band's Midas touch at this point that even film soundtracks caught up in the Take That hype benefited. In August 2007 they released 'Rule the World', the theme tune from the Robert De Niro/Michelle Pfeiffer movie *Stardust*. The song itself was not on the film's soundtrack, but its association with the movie, plus a very polished video featuring clips from the film mixed in with the band – looking as stylish as ever – singing in four separate video booths boosted box office takings sizeably no doubt. Although the single just missed out by one place from topping the chart, it was nonetheless another sign that Take That were, if anything, *bigger* than ever. The song itself was a sublime composition, adding to the growing canon of beautifully crafted songs which have been released since the band returned in 2005. By now, the comeback had turned into a genuine and credible renaissance.

Barlow made no secret of his joy about the ongoing success, happily telling every interviewer that he was just delighted; likewise, Mark Owen would repeatedly say they were proud, delighted and surprised. They clearly enjoyed the experience too, because back in the final week of February 2007 they had announced major plans for an autumn jaunt – heralded as 'The Beautiful World Tour' – kicking off in mid-

November, heading through all the major arenas such as Glasgow SECC, London's O2 Centre and Manchester MEN. In total the bandwagon stopped off at forty-nine cavernous venues around Britain and Europe. Surely they had over-extended themselves and might not sell all the 370,000 tickets? Not so – the tour sold out in less than three hours (there were so many disappointed fans unable to get tickets that dozens of cinemas nationwide screened the shows live to soften the blow). Take That were now one of the very biggest live draws in the world.

Two minor hiccups in an otherwise largely unblemished phase of unmitigated success came in the second half of 2007. Firstly, Howard missed a show in Austria after suffering a collapsed lung in October. Initial reports suggested he would miss three weeks of the hectic European tour, but remarkably he was back on tour with his bandmates for the next gig in Hamburg. Then, only a few weeks later, he was criticized by anti-drugs campaigners for suggesting that if people smoked marijuana instead of drinking alcohol there would be less violence in Britain's late-night city centres (speaking to *Q* magazine in March 2009 he even admitted to taking LSD in his younger clubbing days). He acknowledged the legal status of marijuana was 'a touchy subject' but his opinion was not met warmly by members of organizations such as Mothers Against

Drugs, whose representative Gail McCann called him 'irresponsible'. But any dipping of the band's morale following these two incidents ended when the DVD of the autumn 2007 tour became the fastest-selling music DVD in British retail history.

With the first comeback tour and album a massive success story, anticipation for the next record and a new set of dates seemed to spiral exponentially and reach a new level of fever pitch. Exactly how had Take That done it? Korda Marshall gave me the record

business's view: 'It's great what they have done: firstly they put the work in to create the profile and work the tour; secondly it was a really strong album with great songs. They have worked that album at media phenomenally well, which is no surprise to me, having been involved with them first time around. Although their comeback won't affect the decisions I make with regard to signing new bands, Take That's success is great for pop music, and for music in general. They have proved how successful an act they were at the height of their fame. It is incredibly difficult to come back. There are very few examples of artists who can match what they have done.'

The question on most people's minds by the close of 2007 was, 'Will they continue to perform and record, or was this all one glorious Indian summer?' Even the band didn't seem sure. Jason told Joe Mott of the *Daily Star*, 'After this tour, that might be it, job done. The lads might want to spend time with their families, I might even want to start a family!'

In fact, despite Jason's jovial teasing, plans were already afoot for a new, all-conquering Take That tour and album. Before that, however, there was yet another Brit Awards ceremony to dominate. It would be easy to think that by now the world's best man band had pretty much achieved all they were going to as a re-formed group, and they had certainly exceeded all their initial expectations. Yet somehow Take That managed to ratchet up their profile yet again by being nominated in four categories for the February 2008 Brit Awards. Unlike the previous year, they were given a nod for 'Best Live Act' as well as deserved nominations for 'Best Single' ('Shine'), 'Best British Group' and 'Best British Album'. They scooped actual Brits in the first two categories, beating off stiff competition from acts such as Leona Lewis, Arctic Monkeys, Kaiser Chiefs, Klaxons and Muse.

This notable triumph was complemented in May 2008 when Gary and Howard attended the award ceremony for the prestigious Ivor Novello songwriting awards,

taking home the award for 'Most Performed Work' for 'Shine'. The only major award ceremony they were unable to attend was the newly launched Vodafone-sponsored event that championed live acts, and saw Take That scoop the much-coveted 'Tour of the Year' gong. And why couldn't they attend? Because to the delight of their millions of fans the band were in Los Angeles finishing off their next studio album.

With the band working behind the scenes on their next record, an unauthorized Take That musical called *Never Forget* was planned for the West End of London, and initially Gary Barlow was vehement it would not be allowed to proceed. 'I'm furious and I'll do everything legally possible to stop the show, which has the smell of the end of a pier about it.' However, after hearing posi-

tive reports of the show (which opened in May 2008) from his own friends, Gary's stance softened, and eventually, after lengthy legal discussions, numerous songs by the band were licensed for use in the musical. The show has since proved to be a great success in the vein of other 'tribute' shows such as those about Queen and ABBA. Gary has also suggested that he would himself like to pen an official stage musical about the band's career in the future.

The band's dominance at this point was so complete that there were even whispers about over-exposure, but this theory was completely unsupported by the actual response of the record-buying public. In late October 2008 the band announced a series of huge live stadium shows for the following summer – *The Circus* Live 2009. Even given their own hefty commercial success, the response to tickets being made available was a shock – the 700,000 seats were sold in less than eight hours, making the tour the fastest selling in British music history, usurping the previous record set by Michael Jackson's colossal tour for his album *Bad*. The band's promoter, SJM, said such sales figures were 'totally unprecedented' and pointed out that, during a severe economic downturn, to sell £35 million worth of tickets was phenomenal. Take That were rewriting pop's record books yet again.

Such was their profile that they were honoured with their own *X Factor* show in November 2008, with the excitable contestants meeting Mark and Gary in person and performing hits from the band's back catalogue. The show was an opportunity to see

Gary Barlow at his finest. Standing next to a piano with Mark, he welcomed the various wannabes and talked them through the songs they were to perform. What was striking to watch was how relaxed Gary was: he looked as if he was having a great time and thoroughly enjoying the experience. Some of the contestants were visibly shaken meeting the pair but, as always with Take That, the two superstars were unassuming and very friendly.

Moreover, when the band themselves performed the forthcoming new single 'Greatest Day' (from the fast-approaching new album *The Circus*), they effortlessly sang live. Gary's voice seemed to have reached a new level: technically he can control his vocal range with exact precision, yet he is able to inject enormous emotion into the most difficult melodies. His – and the band's – vocal prowess was in stark contrast to the mimed performance of pop car-crash Britney Spears on a later edition of *X Factor*, a shallow and rather hollow display of lip-synching which drew heavy criticism from, among others, Gary Barlow. 'I don't see the point in Britney any more. She was rubbish on the show. I think she's more famous now than she deserves to be. Why come on a show like that and mime?' Howard agreed: 'All the contestants on the *X Factor* are so talented and were able to sing and dance live. So why wasn't Britney able to do it? It's the whole point of the show, and her miming looked stupid.'

'THE SONG SOUNDED LIKE A CLASSIC ON FIRST HEARING.'

Confirming Gary's long-since renowned ability to write songs in a prolific and precise fashion, in the autumn of 2008 he was involved in one of the funniest television spoofs ever screened. His personal friend, the superstar comedian from Bolton, Peter Kay, had written a scathing parody of the reality TV audition shows with the brief title of *Britain's Got the Pop Factor and Possibly a New Celebrity Jesus Christ Soapstar Superstar Strictly on Ice*, which screened on Channel 4 in October. Kay played the overweight winner of the show, the transsexual Geraldine McQueen, with an unnerving credibility. Indeed, the show was so accurate a spoof that Simon Cowell was said to be greatly annoyed; the week after transmission Geraldine's 'The Winner's Song' hit the No. 2 spot of the actual UK singles charts, co-written of course by one Mr Gary Barlow. This wasn't the last time that Take That worked with Geraldine. For the band's lavishly produced TV special, *Take That Come to Town*, Geraldine reappeared in the audience and was hauled up on stage to fire questions at the band, after which she 'accidentally' fell on top of Mark.

The first signs of Take That's new album material came with the quite stunning late November single, 'Greatest Day'. Once again, the song was a return to the style of 'Back for Good', with gentle acoustic strumming softly leading the listener in. Then came the stabbing piano and Gary's unforgettable vocals. Somehow – like 'Back for Good', 'Patience' and 'Rule the World' before – the song sounded like a classic on first hearing. Once the wave of strings and falsetto backing vocals rush the song towards its climactic crescendo, the emotional power is overwhelming (brilliantly spoofed in an internet clip by Gary Barlow for the birthday of BBC Radio 1 DJ, Chris Moyles). Another massive song from Take That; not surprisingly, another No. 1, replacing Beyoncé at the top and giving them their eleventh chart-topper (to date it has sold 275,000 copies). Anticipation for the new album was becoming startlingly intense.

Meanwhile, the crossing of the band's path with Britney Spears wasn't over after the *X Factor* miming débâcle: it transpired that her own 'comeback' album – released after a highly publicized breakdown and hospitalization that shocked even the scandal-ravaged world of pop – was to share the same title as Take That's: *The Circus* (Britney's was simply *Circus*). Neither act was prepared to alter their album title, but it mattered little to the That-ers, who beat Spears to the top spot when their albums were both released in the first week of December 2008. They had produced yet another chart-topping record to add to the swelling list of achievements since their comeback.

The Circus is a worthy No. 1 record. Notably, the soft piano intro of 'The Garden' showcases Mark's lead singing, another example of the band's four-way split on writing credits and shared vocals. His low register in the opening verse is contrasted brilliantly by Gary's shining chorus vocal, before he hands over to Howard for the second verse. This is a statement of intent – we are Take That, we are a team, a band, a *gang*.

After the anthemic single 'Greatest Day', the album dips somewhat with the odd, rolling, piano-led 'Hello'; like the forthcoming single 'Up All Night', this sister song to 'Shine' was a clear nod to the Beatles and the Fab Four's influence on Gary's song-writing. Then it was back to minor-key piano heaven, with yet more of those devastating Barlow vocals for 'Said it All'. By the time the song crashes into its swirling chorus, the album has already surpassed expectations, another smash hit record. From here on it swoops easily from the jaunty ('Up All Night'/'Here') to the melancholic ('What is Love?'/'The Circus') to the sophisticated pop ('How Did it Come to This?'/'Hold Up a Light'). *The Circus* is an example of accomplished songwriting, controlled yet emotional vocals, crafted lyrics and a lavish soundtrack. Following on from *Beautiful World*, it also confirmed that Take That's career since the comeback was – in terms of songs – far superior to their original incarnation.

'THERE SEEMED LITTLE ELSE TAKE THAT COULD ACHIEVE.'

Beating Britney Spears to the top spot was impressive, but the scale of the success was shocking: the album enjoyed the year's biggest first-day sales of 133,000 copies (toppling Coldplay's *Viva La Vida or Death and All His Friends*); the record also easily beat the first-day sales of its predecessor *Beautiful World*; the momentum did not stall, with the record passing the magic million mark by the second Friday after its release (only *Be Here Now* by Oasis reached the seven-figure mark faster; *Beautiful World* was third after *The Circus*); at the time of writing, *The Circus* has sold over 1.5 million copies and looks set to eventually surpass the 2.5 million copies the band shifted of *Beautiful World*. With the album at No. 1, the single at No. 1 and the forthcoming tour the fastest selling in British history, there seemed little else Take That could achieve.

On a personal note, the winter of 2008 welcomed Mark's second child, when his fiancé Emma Ferguson gave birth to a baby girl called Willow Rose in late November; similarly, Gary and wife Dawn saw their third child, a girl called Daisy, born in January 2009. For the next single, 'Up All Night', Gary is not seen in the later stages of the video, as he had to dash home because Dawn had gone into labour.

This strong family orientation has reinforced Gary's – and the band's – popularity, the man band showing themselves to be family men too. Take this unassuming and very honest quote from a proudly un-rock and roll Barlow: 'Isn't Saturday night busy? You've got *Strictly Come Dancing*, *X Factor* … but *Dancing on Ice*, that's my favourite. I've got to prepare for two years' time, when I'm on it.'

It wasn't just the charts that the band dominated. The newspapers were filled with Take That stories on a daily basis. Gary's mother was reported to be more pleased that her son's band was advertising M&S, her favourite shop, than when he won several prestigious Ivor Novello awards; there was talk of a film about their incredible career being made; Barlow was working on a soundtrack to a major terrestrial TV drama; Jason has been writing a TV soap about music students; Gary had gathered together a group of friends to climb Mount Kilimanjaro for a televised Comic Relief charity special; he had also been in talks about running his own record label, with some suggesting he could be the 'next Simon Cowell' … it seemed there was no limit to the potential. Capping off another triumphant campaign, the band attended the Brit Awards in February 2009, arriving over the stage in a neon spaceship for their performance of 'Greatest Day' (sadly missing out on 'Best British Group' to Elbow).

The band was no longer the story of the biggest comeback in pop history; by 2009 they were, simply, the biggest band in the country.

THE PRODIGAL SON OR A THORN IN THE SIDE?

PART OF THE APPEAL OF Take That as a foursome was their dignified silence in the face of some fairly vile comments by Robbie Williams when his career was supersonic and theirs non-existent. Then, once their comeback had taken the pop world by storm, they resisted any temptation to snipe back at the post-*Rudebox* descent of their former band mate into yet more personal crises. Indeed, Gary even went so far as to partially credit Robbie's own massive career for keeping the Take That flame alive in the hearts of the British public: 'We should thank him because I honestly think if it wasn't for him and for his huge success, there wouldn't still be the interest there for us that has put us back on the map. So cheers, Robbie, thanks a lot.'

'MAYBE ONE DAY IT'LL HAPPEN.'

The band's position on Robbie had initially been that they would welcome a one-off reunion, probably for a song or two, but were not looking for a full-blown return of the maverick pop star. Howard had even said, 'The timing just never worked out. We all still think that maybe one day it'll happen. For us anyway, that'd be the icing of the cake.' By 2007 this had mutated into Mark simply saying, 'We'll have to wait and see if he's up for it … let's just say we're keeping in touch about it.' Even Jason, who was notably reserved in his comments about Robbie, said, 'Maybe it's my romanticism, but I think if we do future albums, it's inevitable Rob will sing with us.' Speaking to Jonathan Ross, Gary then said, 'The door's always open.'

However, the widespread doubts about Take That's success without Robbie had quickly dissipated; by the end of 2007, as mentioned, the general consensus seemed to be that Robbie needed them more than vice versa. Still further, by late 2008, with the band's new tour breaking all records and the album selling so strongly, the ever-growing legions of Take That fans appeared to be urging the band *not* to let Robbie rejoin. They simply didn't need him any more. There was almost a sense that a wave of disappointment would sweep over their fan base if they relented and allowed him to return. And this wasn't just the public's view. Music mogul Simon Cowell commented to *Heat* magazine, 'That's a tricky one. I think I would keep [Take That] as it is. He could do a guest slot now and again. A duet?'

Nonetheless the friction and outright ill-feeling that had previously existed, particularly between Gary and Robbie, was clearly dissolving. Industry gossip suggested that Robbie and Mark had been texting each other, then there was talk of transatlantic phone calls between all five original members, then a possible meeting. It was reported that Mark had 'set up' Robbie and Gary to eat at the same restaurant, sharing dinner at the Chateau Marmont hotel in Los Angeles, where by all accounts the three old friends had a brilliant night and were spotted 'deep in conversation'.

The rumour mill went berserk, with headlines splashed across all the tabloids and even making feature stories on the 'serious' news channels such as Sky and BBC News 24. Gary himself reinforced this with such statements as, 'He said some horrible things about me, but I'm old enough to get over that now. I think that's the beauty of having kids as well: it teaches you that there are things in life that just aren't important.' These were hardly the words of a man refusing to reconcile with his old friend and colleague. The speculation went up another notch. All of the band spoke in the media about regretting not helping Robbie more when he first melted down, with Gary talking to *Q* of 'a series of events we should have spotted. That's my one regret. I missed the signs. I think we all did.' Howard went further, revealing he had since apologized to the star: 'I said I was sorry I never took the time to notice he was drinking a bottle of vodka a day.'

Even Robbie's mum entered the fray, telling the *Sun*, 'I feel that it will happen.' The feverish interest in the escalating saga was only heightened when Gary then seemed to rule out Robbie's full return with outright denials of any reunion; speaking to the *Big Issue* he said, 'When it comes down to it, he's just not going to be in the band again. I just don't think there's a place for him now here.'

The return of Robbie seemed even more unlikely given his recent reportedly erratic behaviour. The tabloids pored over the stories with glee: he was reportedly walking around the streets of LA dressed in a $60 gorilla costume complete with a large pair of black sunglasses, supposedly the first time he'd left his mansion for three months; he was allegedly indulging his love of Ufology to the point of visiting secret locations for spotting extraterrestrial activity; his recent split from a girlfriend was supposedly fuelled by his interest in alien life; he was generally behaving in an unconventional way. Surely he wouldn't rejoin the band now? Besides, he lived 6,000 miles away …

… although not when he was at the football with Gary Barlow. Hastily snapped footage of the two former 'enemies' clearly at ease in each other's company were streamed all over the web and news channels when Williams attended an Arsenal match in November 2008. Once again, the by-now expected denial of a full reunion came from the TT press office. Yet later, on BBC Radio 1, Gary revealed they were all emailing and phoning Robbie and that 'it just felt like we were back in the Nineties'.

'IT JUST FELT LIKE WE WERE BACK IN THE NINETIES.'

The biggest headline was reserved for the day Robbie wrote about the reunion gossip in his own personal blog. 'I'm over the moon for the boys,' he said, before continuing, 'The thing that struck me the most was how much fun they're having. It's more rewarding when you're a gang. Ever since I left Take That I've wanted to be in a band. We got together a lot over the summer. It was amazing. We've all matured a lot since we parted. I'm very pleased to say the differences we've had have just melted away … I celebrated by getting a Take That symbol tattooed on my right arm. I'm proud to know the boys and … I'd love to be in the band again but I've got some unfinished business of my own.'

Until the band perform the summer 2009 tour the speculation will continue. At the time of writing, Robbie Williams has moved back to Britain, having bought a £7 million Wiltshire mansion, further fuelling the rumours. Balaclava-clad trips to bike shops have done little to dampen the disapproving comments about his recent behaviour, but, with Robbie now living back in the UK, who knows what his next move will be? Perhaps a brief slot for a couple of songs at the Wembley shows? Anything more involved would surely detract from Take That's remarkable comeback.

A guest? Maybe.

A member again. Surely not?

AFTERWORD

IN THE FICKLE WORLD OF pop music, hyperbole, bombast and exaggeration are the very air that we all breathe. Bands come and go, tours sell out and records smash in and crash out of the charts. Yet, with frightening rapidity, the memory of a band can leave the mind within weeks, days or sometimes hours of their demise. When these pop bands' legacies are extinguished, it can be brutal.

Brett Andersen of Suede once said, 'Music can be a very humiliating business, but it's worth it in the end.' And that, oddly, seems to say a lot about Take That. From the first moment they pulled on their silver codpieces and lycra shorts, they were battling against the odds. Nigel Martin-Smith single-handedly took a concept that was then unpopular and cumbersome, ignored every obstacle and, through precision management and limitless vision, made it work. You cannot underestimate his contribution to the tale.

The band themselves were relentless. Aside from all the gossip, the splitting up and all the personal paraphernalia that goes with any major act, the five lads in Take That combined a unique chemistry with a staggering work ethic. Not one person I have spoken to in writing this book denies that the band worked as hard as any other pop band they have come across, or harder. Put yourself in a revealing costume at two in the morning in a northern club singing a love song to 300 blokes throwing beer cans at you and you have some idea of what the band have come through. Fast forward to working with Jim Steinman in New York and then on from that to re-form and become one of the biggest-selling acts in history, and you have yourself one hell of a story.

Let's not forget that Take That also gave us Robbie Williams, 'Entertainer to the People', whose career has already been the subject of immense scrutiny and many

books, including two of his own. How, why and to what degree he failed and then succeeded are all inextricably linked to his time with Take That. Furthermore, his emotional distance from his former band-mates meant that his story was for years an estranged, albeit remarkable addendum to their chronicle; then, when the re-formed foursome started to speak with Robbie again and the media went into a 'will he/won't he return?' frenzy, his overpowering personality started to be felt once more, yet this time more as an interesting aside, a distraction from the commercial juggernaut that his former band-mates had become. Will he rejoin? Only time will tell …

Of course, Take That was the boy band that broke the mould: they wrote their own songs, they choreographed their own routines, they contributed to their videos, they conceived their own live shows. More liberal commentators have frequently called The Beatles 'the greatest boy band of all time', and if that is true then Take That are certainly not far behind.

At the very heart of Take That, however, is a pretty simple duality – Gary Barlow's fabulous pop songs spliced with the band's image. The timelessness of tracks such as 'A Million Love Songs' and most obviously 'Back for Good' empowered Take That with the appeal of a classic songwriting band, straight out of the Lieber and Stoller/Lennon and McCartney school. Against the odds, since they re-formed in 2005 they have proceeded to surpass their original songwriting standard with memorable tracks such as 'Patience', 'Rule the World' and 'Greatest Day', reinforcing the notion that Barlow is a national songwriting treasure. He has penned some of the great pop ballads of all time. Combine this with the blend of looks on offer – smouldering, boyish, cheeky and lad-next-door now transformed into sophisticated man band – and you have an irresistible combination. As a nation, millions of us cannot resist. Their chart success speaks for itself.

'TAKE THAT WAS THE BOY BAND THAT BROKE THE MOULD.'

Take That was not just a boy band. Gary, Mark, Howard, Jason and Robbie were part of everyone's lives. Their songs reflected moments in people's day-to-day existence, musical markers that flagged up personal highlights. Their *Greatest Hits* collections are like photo albums full of memories. That is why, I believe, when they announced they were re-forming, the whole country seemed to want to go and see them. It was like being offered the chance to meet old friends again and relive some good times.

For a large chunk of the Nineties, Take That was the biggest pop band in the world. They captured the nation's hearts in a way that only a rare handful of other acts have ever done. If the reaction of the British public and the music business to their reunion is anything to go by, I suspect Take That will be around for some time to come. Remarkable as it sounds, they are bigger now than ever.

First, they achieved the biggest comeback in pop history. Now they are one of the biggest bands in history.

Let's hope that's not the last of it.

INDEX

PICTURE CREDITS